M000207239

Voyage of the SWAMP FOX

A Trawler Cruising Adventure on the Intracoastal Waterway

Mark A. Mentzer, PhD

Copyright © 2019 by Mark A. Mentzer

All rights reserved.

ISBN 978-1-62806-213-7 (paperback)
ISBN 978-1-62806-214-4 (hardback)
ISBN 978-1-62806-215-1 (ebook)
ISBN 978-1-62806-216-8 (ebook)

Library of Congress Control Number 2019935905

Published by Salt Water Media
29 Broad Street, Suite 104
Berlin, MD 21811
www.saltwatermedia.com

Cover and interior photos © Mark A. Mentzer

Dedication

To Swamp Fox and Ramona

&

Nipper Edgar Mentzer 5th

Table of Contents

CHAPTER 1

The Shakedown Cruise

Having enjoyed ownership of some 14 wood boats over the course of 36 years; spending many mornings over coffee and the yachtworld.com site perusing a myriad of classic wood boats and fascinating pictures; and having recently transferred ownership of a classic cruiser to a noteworthy couple; I found myself walking the boat yards and sheds, innocently gazing at a variety of old woodies. Was it time for my next boat project?

⚓ ⚓ ⚓

A Consecution of Boats

I always loved going places in boats. My childhood memories include summers on various lakes in Canada, where my family camped or rented a cabin and a small boat on a lake. We took our Sears 3.5 horsepower outboard, and fished and explored a wide variety of lakes in both Que-

- 9 -

bec and Ontario. As much as the fishing, I loved driving the boat into all the nooks and inlets, and dreaming about living on a lake someday where I could operate my boat, perhaps offering guided fishing and exploration.

I dreamed of traveling great distances by canoe, running a trap line, or becoming an Alaskan tour guide. It felt like my dreams were materializing when my family purchased a Pennsylvania farmhouse next to a lake created by the Fish Commission the year we bought the home. To add to this, my Dad arrived one night with a boat strapped to the roof racks of our Mercury station wagon! I was ecstatic! I still have that boat to this day- a 12-foot flat bottom Wichita aluminum row boat- as well as the Sears outboard motor. So growing up I rowed (no motors allowed) the length of Speedwell Forge Lake when not riding and driving my favorite horse Robbie around the Lakeside trails I constructed.

The next boats were acquired in the 80s and 90s. First was a 16-foot Mad River canoe made of ABS material, followed by a pair of 16-foot Hurricane fiberglass kayaks my kids enjoyed on my childhood lake. These three vessels, along with the row boat, have seen the waters of the Chesapeake Bay and its tributaries, along with various day trips through the eastern shore of Virginia barrier islands.

When I landed my first job out of graduate school at the Westinghouse Advanced Technology Laboratory, I rented a house on the Severn River, a dozen miles up river from Annapolis. With me came the row boat and 3.5 hp outboard, which I launched from the neighborhood docks. Before my first cruise on the Severn, I decided to take a swim in the river. People were sunbathing all along the beach, but interestingly none were in the water on such a hot day.

I walked to the end of a diving board and took the plunge, only to come up with my face and upper body covered in gelatinous slime, which I pawed off my face in order to see straight. I climbed out of the water onto the dock to find the slime I continued to wipe off my body was composed of what concerned onlookers referred to as "sea nettles" or jellyfish. Folks offered me Adolf's meat tenderizer to take away the sting, asked if I was allergic, and demonstrated other signs of genuine concern for my wellbeing. Fortunately I only experienced some minor tingles, and am not allergic to anything that I know of. Thus went my first experience with sea nettles, which dominated the shallow waters on the river that day.

Another new experience for me was a roommate's invitation to share some "Maryland Crabs" he purchased locally- along with instructions on how to crack them and get to the delicious meat- seasoned with "Old Bay" salt and dipped in vinegar. A work colleague later complemented my new-found dietary roster by taking me out on his workboat and teaching me how to tong for oysters. Raw from the half shell, we added some hot sauce to a couple of dozen each, tonged rather easily from the Eastern Bay off Greenbury Creek (coincidentally the location at that time of the Guinness World Record size Bluefin crabs.)

While entertaining my sister and her husband one day on a Severn River beach I transported a load of picnic items to the beach from my community pier and motored back in the 12-foot rowboat with the Sears outboard, where I was overcome by a high-speed motorboat that flew past me, leaving a huge wake. I did not stand a chance, and was capsized along with my load on the way to the beach. Friends swam to me and we collected all the items (the Wichita has floatation under the seats and cannot sink); but unfortunately the Sears went under running wide open, and required lots of attention to get it back in running order. I needed a bigger boat!

The summer of 1981 was quite eventful. Around the time of my capsizing a neighbor placed a For Sale sign on a wooden boat sitting a few houses down from mine. I looked it over, finding it quite interesting. The boat was an old (year unknown) 18-foot Grady White lapstrake with a 65 hp Mercury outboard, off-center steering, and a nicely flared bow. This looked like a boat I could survive in!

I purchased the boat and enjoyed two years in it before the gradually deteriorating transom necessitated a complete repair or another boat. I enjoyed many trips to my friend's place across the bay on Greenbury Creek, near the Wye River, explorations to the mouths of the Severn, Magothy, Chester, and other rivers, and some fairly long-distance cruising for a boat this size. But one weekend driving towards Kent Island I spotted a boat laying on the grass in a boat yard; and I turned in to investigate.

This turned out to be a 1960 Ski Craft boat, built in New Holland, PA, near where I grew up. It was 26 feet, constructed of marine plywood, with a small cuddy space under the console, but no engine and no trailer. I purchased the boat for nearly nothing, donated the Grady White to the Salvation Army, kept the 65 Merc, and the trailer, and hauled the Ski Craft to the home I was renting- this time on Stoney Creek across from the Kennecott Copper Plant near Baltimore.

I installed the 65 Merc, some new steering cables, and completely disassembled the boat in my yard. I then pulled it into a screen-in porch at my rental house, and set up a repair and varnishing operation. I sister-ribbed nearly all of the floor, refastened most of the boat, and completely restored and varnished the boat to near-original condition.

The boat served me well for the next two years- lots

of cruising, an attempt to sleep on the boat but without success as the open cuddy allowed the mosquitos to devour me one night out on the Chester River- and nightly waterskiing weeknights with a neighbor who would take turns driving and skiing. Many nights I would stop with friends at the waterfront bars in Annapolis or on the Magothy River and then ski home. I also took as many as 11 friends on Inner Harbor cruises in this boat. But because of concerns with the sister-ribbed flooring, and a certain "wobble" to the boat, along with the trusty old Merc showing severe signs of trouble, I sold the Ski Craft.

Right on cue, I spotted a 19-foot Elgin fiberglass (!) ski boat with some nice details. I took the boat with me when I moved back to PA for a new job. Up there I trailered the boat to some PA lakes- but after the wide-open freedom of boating on the Chesapeake, I felt very limited and less excited about the type of cruising I had grown accustomed to in MD. So I sold the boat after a year.

Around that same time some friends took me boating on Lake Aldred- part of the Susquehanna River- in their 18-foot Elgin fiberglass tri-hull ski boat with an open bow. I liked the old classic looks of the boat, and the rig where the boat was lifted on a pulley system and rolled out to the water. I ended up purchasing that boat, and enjoyed the scenic Susquehanna for a few years, finally selling the boat after its use tapered off. Prior to selling the boat however, I trailered it many weekends to the Northeast River, and cruised through the C&D Canal, with stops for entertainment in Chesapeake City. This rekindled my interest in the Chesapeake. Thus began a period of marriage, raising children, and much more canoeing and kayaking.

My most memorable canoe trips were with my father. These included several nice spots in the Pocono Mountains, and a canoe tour of 13 trout streams in Vermont during the late 80s. I also kayaked with my children around the bays behind Ocean City MD and Chincoteague Island. I would occasionally row around Speedwell Forge Lake in the row boat, as well as the canoe and kayaks. Short of a cruise to Alaska, my larger-boat cruising took a break through the nineties.

Fortunately, I had a friend with a 23-foot fiberglass fishing/ski boat who loved bar hopping on the bay, and as my children spent weekends away I was able to enjoy getting back on the Chesapeake during the late nineties. When time permitted, I spent morning coffee time perusing the listings on the yachtworld.com site- focusing mainly on old wooden boats- but also deciding on the most logical choice for my next boat. I honed it down to a 28-foot aft cabin inboard/outboard. This provided the ability to sleep overnight, a shower, separate stateroom, and relative fuel economy.

I located such a boat- a 28-foot Sea Ray, in Havre de Grace, inspected the boat, and bought it. I drove it up to a marina in Charlestown MD, kept it there for a year, and then moved across town to the Charlestown Marina. I spent several summers on this boat; and my children really enjoyed "camping out on the water" weekends and longer in the summer. Summer vacations with my kids included trips to Annapolis one year and to St. Michaels the next.

The boat was named *Bad Buoy* by the previous owner- and I kept the name. It ran fairly well most of the time- except during our two vacation cruises. On the first, the prop spun off when I placed it in reverse while docking at our location. And the second year the lower unit on the outdrive fell apart. That year I called for a ride home by car. After locating a lower unit on ebay, my marina installed the parts and I was back in business. But it seemed time for another boat, so I sold the Bad Buoy on ebay and went back to looking at wood boats.

This time I came across a 1970 38-foot Pacemaker with twin 454s (gas engines), generator, a full-size refrigerator in the galley, forward and aft cabins, hot water heater, full shower, two heads, and a salon area with pull-out sofa bed and recliner chair! There were two helms with stairs to an upper bridge above a raised-deck platform- almost trawler-style arrangements. My children and I loved the space; and I enjoyed the maneuverability of twin screws. I could pull down the dual throttles, place one engine in forward and the other in reverse, and turn on a dime! The boat was really a pleasure to operate and "camp" on.

As the boats got larger, the maintenance increased in proportion. I took a slip at the same marina in Charlestown, MD where 29 full-time (year-round) liveaboards resided on four piers on the Northeast River. The mechanics there were happy to winterize and dewinterize the boat for me, at marina rates I was now experiencing more frequently. There were 17 species of spiders and many bats sharing the covered slips; and I had to fight my way through the cobwebs upon arriving at the marina on a Friday night.

Now I experienced my first proper cruising! I could now take groups of friends to places like Chestertown up the Chester River, Tilghman Island, Rock Hall, and other nice spots for a weekend overnighter. Many times my friends left the boat and took rooms in the towns where we stopped. I could run the generator while underway so there was hot water for a shower, and guests could enjoy a cocktail from the bar in the salon. One notable aspect of these trips, however, was the fuel consumption. While I would never accept money from friends for fuel, the boat did not sip its fuel.

At the sweet spot of around 2800 rpms for cruising, with the engines nicely synched for optimum efficiency, the boat drank about 35 gallons per hour. This meant a round trip from the Northeast River to Tilghman Island and back was about an $800 trip! At dockside fuel prices, my fill ups easily exceeded $1000. But these were some memorable trips and loads of fun.

In early November of 2006 my father passed away, four years after my mother. As part of my grieving process I took a drive in my pickup truck with Nipper, the dog I inherited from my father. We traveled the length of the eastern shore to Cape Charles, and began working our way back north, alternating between Oceanside and Bay side. As we crossed over the bridge in Cambridge MD northbound I happened to glance over to the city docks and marina. There was just one boat in the water that late-November day. It looked like perhaps an old Elco or some similar model antique vessel- and I had to turn around and take a look.

I drove along the waterfront streets of the old town and located the docks. I was able to drive right up to the docks, and gave Nipper a little run and some water. I put him back in the truck and walked over to the boat. Just as I began admiring the bright work and 45-foot classic commuter-style lines, the sedan door opened up, a man smiled and said,

"She's for sale!"

I replied, "What year is this boat?" as I walked toward the transom to see the name and hailing port.

I read the name "*OLD DAD*" thinking "what a coincidence and a nice name for a boat!"

The owner Dave replied, "1926- placed in service in 1927."

I was astounded with this information, as that's the year my dad was born! I asked to come aboard. The boat was magnificent- a true classic, maintained in original condition. I stood and admired the sedan/wheelhouse, varnished beams and bright work, chart tables, passageways to the aft master stateroom, forward galley and bunkroom, forward and master heads, red-tiled galley, stove/oven, 671 Gray Marine engine, sedan bench seating, and overall incredible presence of a true classic.

Following lots of enjoyable discussion, a sea trial, survey, and some negotiation, the boat was mine! I knew this one was a keeper, so when the surveyor indicated

> "that shaft log is weeping some water...should
> be ok for another year or so...but at some point
> that will need to be replaced..."

I decided to enlist the services of the local boatyard to replace the shaft log, take the boat down to the wood and apply a 7-coat paint job, and repair the typical list of "small" things suggested by the surveyor. Three weeks later the boat was ready to launch. I stayed in a B&B while inspecting the final work and taking possession of the boat when the marina lifted her in the water. After a few days for the planks to swell shut, I was ready for the cruise north to my slip at the Charlestown Marina, next to the Pacemaker.

About this time, I took a job at the Army Research Lab at the Aberdeen Proving Ground, and decided to live on the boats for a while. I spent a cold winter on the Pacemaker (hot water and shower), on the last two slips on my pier. The river froze over, but my bubbler system kept both boats free from the ice. I shoveled a path through the snow to my car in the parking lot to drive to work. Weekends I commuted home to my PA residence for laundry chores and to pick up my children for the weekends. In warmer weather we often drove back down to the boats, where we enjoyed the local towns and evenings playing cards at the galley table on *OLD DAD*.

I decided to sell the Pacemaker, as *OLD DAD* was certainly the gem of the fleet- and double slip fees was a bit steep. The first potential buyer's surveyor discovered rotten wood in one of the rudder posts, and the deal fell apart. So I pulled the boat and did an extensive repair of the post, learning much about epoxy and specialized wood repair. I disclosed this to potential buyers and was able to sell the boat quickly.

We enjoyed *OLD DAD* for eleven years. Many of those years I took the boat to the Father's Day weekend Antique and Classic Boat Festival in St. Michaels. I look forward to this annual event, as the camaraderie and entertainment is excellent; and many fine boats arrive for the show and contest. *OLD DAD* won "Best of Show" in the cruisers category one year (out of 32 boats) as well as the "Best Restoration" award from the *BoneYard Boats* magazine owner.

I missed the show the past few years because to get there by boat takes at least a full day from where I lived in Virginia; and I did not want to take a day off from my teaching. It's been several decades since I called in sick at any of my jobs. I want to maintain my streak!

The kids grew up and went off to college and careers; and I sold *OLD DAD* to a twenties-era collector. He was interested in the boat for several years and finally decided to purchase her.

Back to my consecution of boats. I next acquired an 18-foot center console with a like-new Yamaha 90-hp outboard. The modified V-hull improves on the pounding and splashing of the locally ubiquitous Carolina Skiffs; and the ability to raise the props helps get the boat through shallow spots at low tide. I enjoyed the boat for local trips to Smith and Tangier Island, and to Captain E's Hurricane

Grill at the mouth of the Pocomoke River, and for stops at the local beaches. But the lure of longer-distance cruising still embraced me; and I found myself perusing the web for wood cruisers during morning coffee.

⚓ ⚓ ⚓

M/V SWAMP FOX

Circumstances placed me in the Chesapeake, VA region, where I happened upon the Atlantic Yacht Basin below Great Bridge on the Albemarle and Chesapeake Canal. I ran into a few owners, some sales and marina guys, and other possible buyers as I spent hours browsing the numerous boats for sale. After boarding an old Egg Harbor and a few other classics, I came upon the boat that really struck me- kind of like sirens in your ears and a multitude of incoherent shouting voices- indicative of the presence of a potential "next boat."

Floating in a winter storage slip was a 1970 Classic Grand Banks. 32-foot length, 11'6" beam, semi-displacement hull with full-length skeg and hard aft chines for stability, wide walk around teak decks, fly bridge, dual-helm chart plotters, radar, VHF radios, autopilots, single screw

Ford Lehman diesel, Onan diesel generator, bow thruster, full galley, forward stateroom, shower, closet storage, air conditioning and heat, great head room, panoramic-view windows, fresh and gray water holding tanks, accessible engine room, dinette and settee, aft deck and fly bridge seating, a Livingston 9-foot dinghy with outboard, and enough bright work to keep the avid wood boater busy between economical cruises at 7-8 knots and 2.5 gph fuel consumption! This is one of the most popular trawlers ever produced, with 861 of this model manufactured in the early years of the Grand Banks factories. Why yes! I scheduled a survey and test drive.

I located some vintage advertising for the Grand Banks 32, which aptly described the boat for

"seasoned yachtsmen....appreciate the rugged functional beauty, born of purpose....1,000-mile range, 17,000 pounds.... beauty of fine teak joiner work and teak parquet cabin soles.... mast and boom hoist aboard dinghies, large fish, air tanks or in a blow carry a steadying sail...spacious 88 sq. ft. teak cockpit... wide walk around teak decks. A built in pole locker, and handy swim step. ....interiors are outstanding– the airy spacious main saloon is inviting with its "L" shaped settee, hi-lo teak table and beautiful golden Burmese teak joiner work. Her beautifully functional galley...well planned interiors are most comfortable..." and so forth.

I researched the Grand Banks 32. Various models and iterations (more than 900 boats) of the 32-foot length were produced from 1965 to 1996. Fiberglass hulls began in 1973. Many owners, owners' associations, user groups, and other boating enthusiasts attest to the remarkable quality and workmanship of these vessels. Teak decks and fuel tanks are often mentioned as high-quality items- which is a great benefit since these can be high-cost items to replace.

After an informative and successful survey and test drive with a reputable wood boat expert, and following a few offers and counteroffers, I finally owned my first trawler- one of the most popular models! Before taking ownership I scheduled some maintenance items with the boat yard at Atlantic Yacht Basin, including a fresh coat of anti-fouling bottom paint, new fuel pump, center windshield wiper motor, new horn, and replacement bridge throttle cables. This all timed nicely with my spring break from teaching high school mathematics, and I scheduled payment and possession for day one of my vacation and a week-long shakedown cruise. I arranged to leave my car at the marina, to be picked up upon my return with the boat to its new home port of Onancock VA. I named the boat SWAMP FOX, which was my father's nickname.

I was accompanied on the voyage by my favorite boating partner, my dog Nipper (Nipper Edgar Mentzer, 5th).

Nipper passed since this last boat trip together. He was in his 18th year- a 75-pound mix acquired from a PA Amish farm by my father, from whom I inherited Nipper a decade ago. Nipper enjoyed this cruise and a final camping trip together, before passing peacefully in his favorite spot looking across the water on my deck north side on Chesconessex Creek in Onancock, Virginia.

He is buried next to the deck, facing the sunsets we enjoyed watching together. That dog really knew how to enjoy life, and he had a great one with my father and me. They are both missed tremendously, and will be in my thoughts as I cruise without their excellent company. We always had a dog named Nipper; and my father was great at locating these dogs. If I acquire another dog, I will have to pick it myself.

Friday April 14, 2017

Arrive

I acquired groceries for the refrigerator and pantry, including all of Nipper's preferred treats and cuisine, his favorite mattress and bedding, and we headed south across the bay bridge tunnel for the *SWAMP FOX*. Nipper always loved car rides, but he sensed this trip was to be even more. He seemed to give me a look of extra appreciation as I led him onto the motor vessel and he settled onto his bed in the saloon.

I left Nipper guarding the boat, and loaded all our provisions aboard, paid my bill at the marina, and boarded for the evening along the bulkhead at the Yacht Basin. A seven-foot water snake laid across the deck blocking me from the boat, and some marina workers pushed it off into the water for me. I do not like snakes!

I maintain an unnatural fear of snakes, after playing with a pet snake belonging to my parents' friends when I was six years old. That was a six-foot black snake which we had outside in the yard while our mothers chatted inside the house. I allowed the snake to wind its way around my arms, over my shoulder, and around my neck.

While not poisonous, these snakes will constrict! This one slowly massaged a tighter and tighter grip around my neck, and I fell to the ground, turning blue. The kids ran in the house, announcing to our mothers, "the snake's killing Mark!" The adults saved me just in time.

Saturday April 15, 2017

Atlantic Yacht Basin, Great Bridge, VA
to Coinjock Marina, Coinjock, NC
approximately 34.2 nautical miles

This was to be what I call a "random cruise" where particular destinations are not pre-planned, but rather selected along the way. This provides maximum flexibility, and with the vessel's capability for anchoring out, it is simply not necessary to make reservations and tie up credit card obligations, thereby imposing undue stress to make a certain distance in time for sunset. We embarked south on the Intracoastal Waterway (ICW), of which the Albemarle and Chesapeake Canal is a part. Much of the voyage would be determined by possible boat issues, weather, and the combinations of weather, wind, tides, and chance, that convolve to determine the day's outcome on the water.

One idea was to cruise the "Albemarle Loop" through the Dismal Swamp and back via the ICW- depending on the specific waypoints, perhaps a 100-mile route. Every marina in the loop offers free slip rentals- a very attractive incentive for cruisers to enjoy the area. However due to recent storm damage, debris, and fallen trees, the Dismal Swamp was closed until further notice and/or availability of funds for reopening by the US Army Corps of Engineers. Operators at the visitor center were not optimistic based on the current federal budgetary spending priorities. So we headed south on the ICW, learning the rudiments of bridge openings and navigation via chart plotters, charts, and GPS reckoning, as a check against the well-marked channel system.

The weather was brisk and sunny, waters were calm for most of the way, and we got a good feel for the boat, driving from the fly bridge. Nipper napped his way along the route in his sedan station- snacks and water available as he liked.

⚓ ⚓ ⚓

Sunday April 16, 2017

Coinjock Marina, Coinjock, NC

With questionable conditions on the Albemarle Sound for the next few days, Nipper and I spent Easter in Coinjock, organizing the boat, and enjoying the friendly boaters coming and going at this popular stop on the ICW. Nipper was his usual pleasant self, but it was clear the trip was a bit of a struggle for him. His walking had declined to the point where I needed to carry him on and off the boat for his walks, and he was increasingly unsteady on his feet.

While he recovered almost fully from his stroke a year ago, he was in declining health. It was clear however, he was enjoying the trip as much as he did cruising on our previous boat, the 45-foot antique motor cruiser *OLD DAD*.

The decision was to either continue southward, out into the Albemarle Sound and perhaps over to Manteo, or to head back north for the cruise up the bay to Onancock. With the weather conditions on the Sound still sounding a bit hazardous for a boat I was not yet familiar with, I decided to turn north.

⚓ ⚓ ⚓

Monday April 17, 2017

Coinjock Marina, Coinjock, NC
to Sunset Boating Center, Hampton, VA
approximately 51.2 miles

This was a long day of cruising, considering my learning curve for the boat, its cruising characteristics, and the heavily-trafficked route through the Norfolk shipyards area. The marina was quite small; and the highlight was the barbeque shack at the end of the docks.

⚓ ⚓ ⚓

Tuesday April 18, 2017

Sunset Boating Center, Hampton, VA
to Salt Ponds Marina, Hampton, VA
approximately 8.5 miles

This was a very rough-weather cruise to Salt Ponds, Hampton, VA. Nipper became quite anxious as we encountered huge random waves. A spray can cap wedged itself under one of the bilge pump switches, unknown to me, causing one of the pumps to run continuously. While it was not logical that only one pump ran, for a few minutes I thought I was taking on water. I headed toward shore and managed to find the inlet to Salt Ponds, barely making it past the rocks. I tied up in high gusting winds.

⚓ ⚓ ⚓

Wednesday April 19, 2017

Salt Ponds Marina, Hampton, VA

Waiting at Salt Ponds for better weather gave Nipper and me a chance to relax, enjoy the boat, and do some reading for a few days.

⚓ ⚓ ⚓

Thursday April 20, 2017

Salt Ponds Marina, Hampton, VA
to Chesconessex Creek, Onancock, VA
approximately 74 miles

The Bay calmed significantly, and we cruised a long reach to Chesconessex Creek, my new home port for *SWAMP FOX*. I was quite satisfied with the shakedown cruise, and looked forward to a variety of cosmetic improvements I planned in advance of a long-range cruise on the Intracoastal Waterway.

CHAPTER 2

The Second Cruise

The boat is documented with the US Coast Guard, insured by Boat US/Geico, covered for Boat US towing, and registered with MMSI. I named the boat *SWAMP FOX*, in memory of my Dad's nickname used by his best friends, and the name by which I sometimes addressed Nipper as well. I installed new name and port of call placards, changed the oil, re-caulked a portion of the teak decks where I suspected leaking, engaged in a thorough cleaning inside and out, repaired a leak in the hot water line to the shower, acquired some decorative pillows for the salon, read some diesel engine manuals, opened some clogs in the deck drainage system, cleaned out the lazzerette, fixed some various electrical issues, hung four flags, tested all components, and tried out the dinghy system before embarking on a longer shake-down cruise.

Much of the early summer was tied up with a variety of obligations related to education. I agreed to teach a summer school math course at Nandua High School, which ran about five weeks, through the month of July. I also teach online graduate systems engineering and computer science courses each semester, including the summer term, for University of Maryland University College (UMUC); and I took four online graduate mathematics courses this summer, as part of another master's degree, at Western Governors University. Several students and parents also enlisted my private tutoring services through WyzAnt for SAT prep, math remediation, reading comprehension, and writing. Finally, my publisher CRC is anxious to receive the draft of my next technical book on the subject of mild traumatic brain injury.

The summer flew by, with added time consumed in repairs to my dock, staining my deck, landscaping yard work, and organization of the personal library I built over my barn. With the exception of two weekend camping trips in my Winnebago, I would not call this "summer vacation," despite what people say about school teachers! Saturday night after midnight, as I wrapped up some grading on student papers in the graduate class I taught, I made a decision! It was time for the next cruise of the *SWAMP FOX*!

So I grabbed a couple of boxes, filled them with canned goods, some bread and snacks from my kitchen, packed some clothes, and planned to roll out in the *Fox* in the morning. Not a lot of planning- but I keep my boats ready to roll at such a moment's notice. With Nipper recently deceased, it was an easy matter to jump in the boat and go. Nipper seemed to really enjoy our camping and boating expeditions. He is sorely missed.

⚓ ⚓ ⚓

Sunday July 30, 2017

Chesconessex Creek
to Cape Charles Yacht Center, Cape Charles, VA
approximately 45 miles

After checking the oil, preparing my lines, loading the refrigerator, and making the bed, I steered the *FOX* out of her berth on Chesconessex Creek and headed south. I stopped in the nice little town of Cape Charles, where the marina provided a golf cart for tooling about the town's shops and taverns.

Monday July 31, 2017
Cape Charles Yacht Center, Cape Charles, VA
to Marina Shores Marina, Virginia Beach, VA
approximately 29.4 miles

After passing under the Chesapeake Bay Bridge tunnel I took a wide arc into the ocean and then tacked back to the entrance to the Virginia Beach inlet. The bridge over this inlet was under construction and the entrances were partially blocked, making it difficult to pass under without hitting the side of the entrance. I proceeded into a highly developed area. There is a great bar and restaurant at the marina where I enjoyed happy hour.

⚓ ⚓ ⚓

Tuesday August 1, 2017
Marina Shores Marina, Virginia Beach, VA
to Deltaville Marina, Deltaville, VA
approximately 52 miles

This was a long day of cruising. I made it to the marina just in time to run through the woods on a path to the nautical museum I'd always wanted to visit. The attendants were very nice and stayed open an extra half hour for me to have a good look around.

⚓ ⚓ ⚓

Wednesday August 2, 2017
Deltaville Marina, Deltaville, VA
to Zahnisers Yachting Center, Solomons Island, MD
approximately 74 miles

I cruised up to Onancock and saw the Chesapeake Buy Boat flotilla; then continued on to Zahnisers. Several hours were lost as I changed course southwest of Tangier Island to avoid the large restricted area.

⚓ ⚓ ⚓

Thursday August 3, 2017
Zahnisers Yachting Center, Solomons Island, MD

Solomons is a great cruising destination. The town features a marine science museum and lots of interesting shops and restaurants. I was greeted at my slip by able dockhands and a nice sign that read, "Reserved *SWAMP FOX!*"

⚓ ⚓ ⚓

Friday August 4, 2017
Zahnisers Yachting Center, Solomons Island, MD
to Hinckley Yacht Services, Oxford, MD
approximately 33 miles

Tides, wind, and sea converged in a perfect day, seemingly tailored to the direction I was headed in a manner that expedited the trip to one of my favorite little towns of Oxford MD. Since my last stop there nearly a decade ago the town has grown tremendously, along with new waterfront bars and restaurants with live entertainment.

⚓ ⚓ ⚓

Saturday August 5, 2017
Hinckley Yacht Services, Oxford, MD

I spent some time replacing a windshield wiper, removing some old lettering on the dinghy, and cleaning the boat interior. Then it was time to explore the town, including an old book store.

⚓ ⚓ ⚓

Sunday August 6, 2017

Hinckley Yacht Services, Oxford, MD
to Dennis Point Marina, St. Mary's MD
approximately 65 miles

I enjoyed a pleasant day's cruise across the bay to St. Mary's, Maryland.

⚓ ⚓ ⚓

Monday August 7, 2017

Dennis Point Marina, St. Mary's MD

Rain day, bad cruising weather, including a tornado warning in the middle of the afternoon dictated another day in Oxford exploring the quaint homes and waterfront attractions. This gave me time as well to contemplate the next stop on the voyage. I decided to cruise up the St. Mary's River, as I always heard it is a nice tributary off the mouth of the Potomac. I arrived at Dennis Point Marina and campground to find the restaurant and store were closed the next day. After a refreshing dip in the pool it was time for some relaxation in preparation for the return to Onancock.

⚓ ⚓ ⚓

Tuesday August 8, 2017
Dennis Point Marina, St. Mary's MD to Onancock, VA
approximately 51.6 miles

It was time to return to home port for some work on the deck caulking project and to prepare for the oncoming school year. *SWAMP FOX* proved a very seaworthy vessel in the shakedown cruises, with many fine features to enjoy. I began planning a cruise to Florida on the Intracoastal Waterway- the trip I longed for over many years.

CHAPTER 3

Preparation for the Intracoastal Waterway

Saturday March 24, 2018

Onancock, VA to Cape Charles Yacht Center

52 miles

Winter took a toll on the above-deck paint job of the prior boat owner. While some of this work could have been accomplished last fall, I remained focused on the deck recaulking above the leaks that woke me during the shakedown cruise. This was very time-consuming work which could be expedited with the use of my recently purchased Fein Tool Multimaster for reefing out the deck caulking as well as the initial sanding of recaulked decks.

I planned to pull the boat at Cape Charles Yacht Center, paint the bottom and sides, and stage the boat for the trip south beginning late June after school graduation. I departed my slip in Onancock and journeyed south seven hours to Cape Charles.

⚓ ⚓ ⚓

Sunday March 25, 2018
Cape Charles Yacht Center

I spent considerable time cleaning the bilge, organizing my paint and restoration materials, and preparing to pull the boat for bottom painting. I converted the sedan bench seat into two bunks for storage down below of all the materials for my floating project at sea.

A bit of anxiety accompanied the trip to Cape Charles, as this marked the start of final preparations for the "trip south" when school lets out in June. Despite all my reading on the subject, it is just too difficult to accurately predict how far I can go on the Intracoastal before needing to turn around in order to start school in late August. I have about ten weeks for the total voyage.

I compiled a list of small chores as part of the preparation for the big cruise. I like to work from lists and to constantly prioritize as part of efficiently working through goals.

- Repair center windshield wiper and repair engine temperature gauge (or sender unit?)- remove instrument panel
- Bottom and side paint at Cape Charles Yacht Center

- Fix dinghy engine bracket and start outboard engine
- Begin a top-to bottom paint job on the upper deck
- Varnish the rails

⚓ ⚓ ⚓

Monday March 26, 2018

Cape Charles Yacht Center

There is always something on my list to work on as with a house. But I enjoy being on the boat and the water, and too often my ambitious maintenance plans give way to simply relaxing on the boat. This is spring break at the school where I teach; and I am pushing myself to complete numerous tasks in parallel with the boat preparation, including grading papers for the two graduate engineering/computer science classes I teach online for University of Maryland University College, completing my final course for the MA Mathematics at Western Governors University, preparing a web site for accessing color photos accompanying this book, and progressing on my fourth technical book- this one on mild traumatic brain injury. I must also complete my taxes before heading back to school in a week.

It has been quite cold sleeping on the boat, as I left my small cabin heater on the last boat when I sold it (another is on the way). While the boat has a built-in heater, it does not keep the boat sufficiently warm in near-freezing temperatures- especially considering the strong draft along the main doorway. I purchased a small standalone heater to augment the built-in unit.

⚓ ⚓ ⚓

Tuesday March 27, 2018
Cape Charles Yacht Center

I drove the boat onto the marina travel lift. I hired the marina to pull and block the boat, power wash, paint the bottom and sides with the paints I provided, replace all the zincs, and lift me back in the water. Today they did the power wash and blocked the boat. We expect two warm days Wednesday and Thursday; and they plan to paint Thursday. I prefer to paint the boat myself, but was told the new regulations require all painting to be done by the marina.

I decided not to sleep on the boat on the hard, and drove back to Onancock for the evening to complete some school work. This turned out to be a very busy working vacation, but a great opportunity to wrap up several long-running projects. Tomorrow I plan to travel to the boat to remove the instrument panel in hope of resolving both the faulty wiper switch as well as the water temperature gauge which has pegged on high.

⚓ ⚓ ⚓

Solo Man, aka Jack van Ommen

Currently residing on his sailboat while making repairs from a wreck off the local barrier islands is author and circumnavigator Jack van Ommen. A native of Amsterdam Holland, Jack has led a full and interesting life. I am reading his latest book documenting his travel to more than 50 countries and including numerous ocean crossings in his 30-foot wooden sailing vessel Fleet Wood. Unfortunately, he has wrecked his sailboat twice while solo sailing at night. Autopilot must be used with precaution!

Wednesday March 28 to Monday April 2, 2018
Cape Charles Yacht Center

Spring break from my school teaching passed quickly as I finished detailing the outside of the boat, including prepping and painting the sides. I continued working my list of repairs and restorative tasks when we placed the boat back in the water. I secured a slip for at least six months at the Cape Charles Yacht Center where the travel lift is located.

Excitement continued to mount as I planned and prepared for the summer voyage. After painting the bottom and sides and returning to the water, my plans and preparations included:

- Changing the oil in the main engine, generator, and oil pump
- Continuing the recaulking of the decks and exploring whether the addition to my tools of a Fein tool multimaster will speed the work of a reefing knife to remove the old caulk
- Painting and varnishing the entire topsides, replacing fuel, water, and oil filters
- Repairing a small leak under the head sink
- Rechecking the shaft log drip rate
- Repairing the back deck drainage system
- Installing solar powered vent fans

- Troubleshooting the center wiper motor
- Replacing transmission fluid
- Locating a manual for the Onan generator
- Installing an icemaker
- Installing a thruster motor zinc omitted in the boat yard schedule

The next three weekends were spent on the boat, working the list, and interjecting some interesting exploration of the town of Cape Charles, VA. The town appears to be experiencing economic surge of the type envied by other small waterfront towns of the eastern shores of MD and VA. Contrasts abound, with a working harbor next to the new mega-yacht center, small shops and the Fuji horseshoe crab bleeding facility (biomedical applications), and several pubs and music venues.

One day near the end of April I was standing in the engine room, bleeding air from the fuel lines out of several release plugs subsequent to changing the fuel filters. It was a calm day and the boat sat peacefully in her floating dock slip. Unbeknownst to me, a recently launched boat attempting to exit the harbor lost an engine and rapidly drifted toward my boat. Two marina hands and one or more occupants of the out-of-control boat shoved off the starboard side of my boat in order to avoid a collision.

The sudden lateral force not only rocked my boat; it

provided sufficient rapid tilt to tip over the heavy engine hatch cover leaning against the side of the upper compartment- right onto my forehead! It felt like I was struck by a baseball bat; but somehow I was not knocked unconsciousness. Blood covered the hatch floor, my face, and shirt. For a few moments I could not tell if it was my nose, mouth, or what was the source of the blood. I was told I needed stitches- but a few properly-placed butterfly bandages did the trick and I got back to work. I'll never simply prop up the engine hatches, as you never know when flat-calm waters can turn rogue and create flying objects!

The next two weekends brought long exhausting days working on my list of items. My objective was to perform preventive maintenance for the long trip south and to embark on or about June 20- the last day of spring! Six-and-a-half weeks to go! I am now at the point where I have a small list of items I'd like the marina mechanic to address in my presence, so I can better understand the engine and be ready should I need to make repairs underway.

I see from my teacher calendar I will have eight weeks for the summer cruise; and my goal is to make it to Florida and back. Many cruisers indicate they do the trip down in ten days. But I want to enjoy the routes and not feel pressure to "make time," thereby missing much along the way. The rough plan is to turn around at 4 weeks and return north.

⚓ ⚓ ⚓

40 Days to Departure!

I'm sitting in my office during planning period at school, thinking about what remains for the preparations. I acquired a "GlocalMe G3 4G LTE Mobile Hotspot, Worldwide High Speed WIFI Hotspot with 1GB Global Initial Data, No SIM Card Roaming Charges International Pocket WIFI Hotspot MIFI Device)" on Amazon. I will test this weekend to determine if this provides the internet access I'll need on the long cruise.

I cannot depend on the local WIFIs at marinas along the way, as I'll be teaching an online course while underway. I want to avoid weak and unsecure signals. I am very fortunate to serve as adjunct Associate Professor of Engineering for an online university, teaching engineering and computer science courses. I will check in with my class asynchronously every day possible; as I like staying on top of student discussions and any questions they may have as they complete their assignments, projects, and exams.

I also want to be sure to check into my automatic bill pay system and online banking services. My next acquisition will be a do-it-yourself home security system, along with at least one scanning camera for my home and library. I decided to first determine the level of connectivity I'll achieve on the boat, before investing in additional remotely-viewed security equipment.

The weather looks promising this weekend, so more epoxying, prepping and painting are in order. I look forward to these weekends, as any time on the water, even while working, is quite enjoyable. My weeks during the school year are filled with lesson planning, teaching, grading, and talking with students. I'm using that famous "teacher time off" in the summer to maximum benefit this year. My plan is to leave the day we're off from school, and to return shortly before school starts back. This gives me more than 8 weeks to voyage south and back.

I must decide whether to haul the outboard along with the dinghy. I envision anchoring out every few nights, where it may often not be necessary to come ashore at all. And when I do come ashore it may be close enough for rowing in without the need for an outboard. This question also begs the issue of registration of the motorized vessel, additional personal property taxes, and carrying gas in a portable tank through the trip. I may take a row around the harbor this weekend as I make the decision regarding the outboard.

⚓ ⚓ ⚓

21 Days to Departure!

Preparations and boat restoration progressed nicely the past few weekends. I took one of my personal days off from school to make a four-day weekend over Memorial Day. Recent accomplishments include installation of a new wiper motor compliments of Atlantic Yacht Basin, replacement of the aft bilge pump, installation of a new water temperature sender unit, cleaning the raw and fresh water strainers, changing out the transmission fluid, changing the fuel pump motor oil, and fiber glassing a few areas where prior window leaks caused some wood damage. All bad wood was removed and multi-layer fabric and epoxy used to repair the wall structure. I also completed the majority of the painting of the entire boat.

The air conditioning prime must be debugged; and a replacement impellor installed. Finally, the generator oil and filters will be replaced, and the SWAMP FOX will be ready for departure. I am studying security systems I can install and monitor while underway- and this is a priority if it is to happen in time. I added an ice maker and plan for an extra cooler on the back deck. A solar shower bag should come in handy for use on the back deck or swim platform as well.

I removed the heavy ten-horse outboard, having decided to row the dinghy when it is needed for trips to shore from anchor points. It placed a lot of weight on the swim platform, and made launching the dinghy more difficult. After removing the outboard I refastened and reinforced the swim platform section taking most of the weight. Then I took a row around the Cape Charles harbor to get a better feel for the dinghy.

The deck recaulking project remains. After spending more than 30 hours on the forward starboard section I acquired a Fein tool to assist in the caulk removal. I plan to do the same section port side in the near future. My goal is a totally watertight boat, with proper ventilation throughout. To that end I installed four solar powered vent fans in key areas aft around the cockpit. I'm thinking about how to best ventilate the forward head area as well.

Work will continue during the trip and as needed. I will also need time some evenings for the online class I'm teaching; and of course plenty of time for writing, relaxing, and enjoying the trip. I plan to take lots of pictures.

⚓ ⚓ ⚓

16 Days to Departure!

The past weekend was quite productive. I arrived to find the air conditioning unit was kicking on and off. I diagnosed failure of the water pump and spent 2 hours disassembling the pump, reseating the bushings, cleaning the impellor, and successfully restoring the AC. I completed some reinforcement of the swim platform and applied teak oil to the entire area. I also removed an old rusted bracket, and sanded and varnished the area where the bracket was located.

I experimented with a different epoxy filler and repaired a small area in the outside rear cabin. Then I completed the paint job on the front of the boat. Sunday it rained off and on the entire day, but I used the time to replace the engine impellor and to replace the oil in the generator. At this point my list of maintenance, repairs, and restoration is almost complete. I plan to paint the bottom of the dinghy, as three days in the water produced visible growth. I happen to have a quart of dark-blue bottom paint that will work just fine.

I feel great satisfaction in having completely painted

the boat inside and out, repaired, replaced, upgraded, and serviced every aspect of the boat. I am cautiously optimistic the SWAMP FOX is ready for the voyage south to Florida. I feel fortunate to own this boat, as it fits my needs perfectly for the type of cruising planned this summer; and the boat should hold its value quite well. The original Ford Lehman diesel engine has about 1200 hours; and should be good for fifteen to twenty thousand more! Now that the boat is fully restored, maintenance costs should be comparable to those for a fiberglass boat. When Grand Banks discontinued this size yacht a few years ago its price was $200,000; and this model brings between $40,000 and $65,000 depending on the boat's condition. The Grand Banks Company continues to prosper since its inception in 1956.

I just accepted a position at a private college prep school in Salisbury. This will allow me to stay on the boat weeknights, and further ensure the diligence required to maintain the boat's excellent quality condition. Five minutes from my new school is the head of the Wicomico River and marina with showers and laundry. The Wicomico has deep water its entire 16-mile length, and offers quite reasonable monthly and yearly dockage and live aboard. This will spare me the 90-minute drive to my home on the Chesconessex Creek.

The route down "the ditch" as the inter-/intra-coastal

waterway is often called, is marked at Norfolk, VA at Mile 0, and ends at Mile 1095 in Miami. Just north of Miami is the turnoff for the Okeechobee Canal, which traverses Florida to the gulf coast. With 8 weeks and six days off from school my plan is turn around and head back north no later than halfway into the trip. Barring unforeseen problems, this should land me somewhere in Florida!

Of the 130+ bridges along the Norfolk to Miami route, about 85 of them must open for boats to proceed through. There is also a lock in Great Bridge, VA. The option to take the Dismal Swamp Canal includes two locks as well. While there are no tides in the stretch from Great Bridge to Morehead City, NC, eight- to nine-foot tides must be accommodated in Georgia. Hot and humid is the forecast for the summer!

While most hurricanes occur during the fall, the season runs from June to November. Careful attention to weather conditions is essential for many reasons. I anticipate good internet connection and will of course rely on the VHF radio as well. Many would advise heading north in the summer and south in the winter. So perhaps next summer's voyage will be north to Maine or Vermont!

I always enjoy covering a distance when I travel. After many bicycling trips all over the state of Vermont, I decided to bike from Bar Harbor, Maine to Lake Placid, New

York one summer with a self-contained bicycle camping group from Montana called Bike Centennial. They provided great low-traffic maps and coordinated signups. About fifteen of us (to start) met at the state park in Bar Harbor and headed out. We shared on a rotating basis the acquisition and cooking of an evening meal at the camp spot, and washing the dishes.

This was a great trip, covering eleven days of beautiful scenery and some challenging rides up and down the mountains- especially the route up to Lake Placid. Employment and other commitments prevented me from continuing across the country, but for years I pieced together routes that will ultimately join together as a complete crossing of the United States. One such memorable trip was a two-week ride from San Francisco to Reno, Nevada (and back).

So the opportunity to travel the east coast via the *Intracoastal Waterway* is of equal interest and value to me. That old saying about "teachers have the summer off!" is partially true- as I have eight weeks and six days in which to accomplish my summer voyage in the *SWAMP FOX*. Many variables will reveal themselves, as wind, weather, tides, obstructions, and mechanical failures may all potentially impact the time factor. Four weeks is a reasonable time at which I must turn around and head north to arrive in time to start my new teaching position.

This weekend over three days I will complete all the items on what seemed at times an insurmountable schedule of maintenance, repair, and restoration. I enjoy being on the water, even if it's to work on the boat. There's a feeling of relaxation I don't enjoy simply sitting on my back deck- despite the beautiful views of Chesconessex Creek, VA. Taking the last of my personal days tomorrow, I look forward to another weekend putting the finishing touches on the Fox.

Not that the work is ever finished with any boat- or with any home. There's always something to work on, repair, maintain, or update. But when you're ahead of the curve with a boat, the work becomes even more enjoyable, as there is always an end in sight. Finishing the recaulking of the decks is the remaining large project at this time; and I hope to accomplish this in pieces during the journey- perhaps a few hours in the evenings when time permits. All of the materials I'll require are stowed onboard the Fox. Otherwise the decks will wait for the fall in the new location at Port of Salisbury Marina.

9 Days to Departure!

I took the last of my personal days from school to make another three-day weekend. The dinghy now has bottom paint; and all of the bright work is newly varnished. I placed one last order with Jamestown Distributors for the materials I anticipate needing on the voyage. This weekend will be the last of the preparations for departure a week from Wednesday- June 20. This is the last week of school, with two "professional days" next week. I will return to a slip on the Wicomico River before starting my new teaching job in Salisbury this fall. This provides much to look forward to for the coming year.

CHAPTER 4

Embarkation!

Tuesday June 19

School is finally over for the summer! I signed out of the building, handed in my badge and computer, thus ending my final stint in the public school systems- looking forward to more industrious and respectful kids at my new private-school position in Salisbury, MD.

My good friend Nick Bohidar (Mr. Bo) provided transportation to the Cape Charles Yacht Center. I enjoyed the full realization of the school year completion and tomorrow's departure southwest across the Chesapeake, to mile marker zero of the Intracoastal Waterway!

Small storms are predicted the next few days, but without high winds or waves. I set the alarm for 5 am, as daylight is 5:40 am- a good time to head across the bay. That gives me time for coffee, the marine weather forecasts, and embarkation!

A note on statute vs nautical miles:

While my Chesapeake Bay charts are in nautical miles, the ICW charts are in statute miles. One statute mile equals 0.869 nautical miles [and one nautical mile equals 1.1508 statute miles.] Because most of the trip is on the ICW, I will make the conversion and report all mileage in statute miles. Many of the ICW landmarks are known by their "mile markers" in statute miles. This is another good reason to report everything in statute miles.

In keeping with another convention, I have expressed boat speed in knots. A knot is a nautical mph. One knot per hour equals 1.15 statute miles per hour. A nautical mile equals 1 minute of latitude and is based on the circumference of the earth. The term knot comes from the 17th century sailing practice of timing the payout of equally-spaced knots from the back of a vessel to calculate the ship's speed in "knots."

Wednesday June 20, 2018
  Cape Charles Yacht Center to Coinjock Marina
  Coinjock, NC- approximately 81 miles

SWAMP FOX cruised nicely at 1800 rpm, averaging about 6 knots/hour, due to delays at several bridges and a lock. Unhindered, she travels easily at 7 knots; and with the right wind and currents she sometimes makes 8 knots and a bit more. A number of no-wake zones slowed the trip. But after more than 13 hours of cruising, today's 80.6 miles brought me to Coinjock Marina, NC! Nipper and I turned around just after this point (ICW mile marker 50) based on severe weather reports and our lack of full knowledge of the boat a year ago.

After the seemingly never-ending complex of the Norfolk Naval Ship Yard, I finally entered the beautiful landscape leading to the first of the bridges that must be opened in order for boats to pass through. This was the Gilmerton Bridge at MM 5.8, followed three miles later by the Steel Bridge. The Great Bridge Lock at MM 11.5 was delayed due to a tug pushing a barge. The lock operators had a tough time getting the tug and barge properly secured in the lock, resulting in more than a half-hour delay. Half a mile further The Great Bridge opened without delay. The highlight of this portion of the trip was a dolphin display just as I entered the Norfolk area.

I entertained previous thoughts of spending the first night out at the free municipal bulkhead in Great Bridge. But the day was going so well, the weather was threatening but still nice, so I continued on- as it turned out, for another 40-some miles. An eagle siting on a dead tree branch stared at me as I meandered down the canal. More bridges (they are all similar in nature), threatening thunder showers, and finally a light downpour as I entered the long crossing of the Currituck Sound, took me to late afternoon. A perfect rainbow crossed the sound in front of my progress for nearly an hour. I briefly considered anchoring out in the sound, but decided to press on to Coinjock and their excellent restaurant.

I am sitting on the FOX typing away as thunderstorms promise to continue into the evening but finish for tomorrow's departure to the Albemarle Sound and the Alligator River. I may do a pump out and replace the Coinjock tree shirt I bought here last year and have worn out. This evening just before the thunderstorms began I tried out my new solar shower. It works quite well mounted on the mast boom. I prefer this to the marina bath houses. I avoided frightening anyone by showering in my bathing suit. Between my Kindle and several dozen books I brought with me, the evenings provide some great reading time.

⚓ ⚓ ⚓

Thursday June 21, 2018
Coinjock Marina, Coinjock, NC to Belhaven, NC
85 miles [166 total]

I departed Coinjock at 8:30 on two-foot waves. After crossing the Albemarle Sound, the Fox proceeded down the Alligator River and Canal and the Pungo River and Canal. After hearing from various boaters of the treacheries of the Albermarle Sound, I was pleased with such a pleasant crossing. No gators were spotted, but two deer returned my glances at the canal's edge. The remote parts of this trip thus far have been spectacular. I enjoy watching the landscape roll past as I meander my way down the ditch. Today there were lots of pelicans sitting on navigation markers, watching the boats go by.

Crossing under the Alligator River Bridge at 1pm, the marine forecast was 93 degrees with a chance of rain and thundershowers. Wanting to buy some time for the overall trip on the days where I could log lots of miles, I continued on. At 7pm the rain started quite suddenly. I enjoyed the new wiper motor with intermittent feature, just as the left wiper stopped working. Thunder, lightning, and high winds and chop added to the suspense, as I crawled my way to an anchorage off the Belhaven canal. But after four tries, I could not get the anchor to set, and finally resorted to tying off on a bulkhead for the evening.

Violent lightning and thunderstorms lasted from about 7:30 to 4am, making it tough to sleep. The rain finally subsided in time for a 5:30 departure sans coffee. But it turned out to be a productive day.

⚓ ⚓ ⚓

Friday June 22, 2018
Belhaven, NC to Dudley's Marina, Swansboro, NC
94 miles [260 total]

Despite early visages of ominous weather, I departed for what turned out to be a 12-hour cruise. After proceeding down the Pungo River, I crossed the Pamlico Sound and River, along with the Bay and Neuse Rivers. There was lots of open water, making it easy to navigate with the automatic pilot, and simply making slight corrections as I traversed long swaths of water. But the latter part of the day portended the nature of the next segments of the voyage with long narrow canals. The narrow passageways necessitated mostly "hands on the wheel" piloting.

Continuing on the Adams Creek and Canal, the

weather improved through the day, so I kept cruising and enjoying the sites along the passageway. The stretch of passage along the edge of Morehead City below Beufort reminded me of the beaches and sandbars frequented by friends on the VA Eastern Shore. Across the channel from my bulkhead slip in Swansboro is a twenty-some foot-high collection of sand dunes. Beyond the other shore line is the North Atlantic Ocean. I gazed briefly at an ocean inlet today during a brief period of confusion traversing the congested throughway.

Next up in the morning I'll possibly make it as far as Wrightsville Beach, NC, and shortly thereafter, Myrtle Beach SC. Thus far the boat is running beautifully. I am confident I may see Florida's ICW as soon as nine or ten days from now- weather permitting. People remind me this is hurricane season; and the idea is to cruise north from May/June to September/October and then head south! I guess they're not school teachers. My hope is that a hurricane will not start to develop in the next few weeks, so that I will have turned around (perhaps the four-week mark) and can escape the storm while heading back northward. Maybe Vermont next summer!

Saturday June 23, 2018

Dudley's Marina, Swansboro, NC
to South Harbor Marina, Southport, NC
82 miles [342 total]

Departed in strong winds at 5:45 am as a fishing tournament swarmed the dock with boats for registration. The tournament director helped me get the Fox away from the dock as strong winds prevented a simple push away. There was also a shoal right next to my boat, which they told me about on the radio after I scraped bottom coming in.

At the New River Inlet (to the ocean) the passageway is wide but confusing. At MM 245, a string of "red rights" became a "red left" for me and a "red right" for boats returning from the ocean. So I went left and hit bottom. Fortunately, I progressed into deeper water and could continue on. The confusing red buoy was even spaced in the same pattern as those for the inland stretch, hence adding to the confusion.

The chart at MM245 reads

"CAUTION NEW RIVER INLET The entrance and delta channels are subject to change. The buoys are not charted because they are frequently shifted in position."

Caution indeed! I could have easily entered the ocean by mistake.

Relative humidity was 96%, temperature 85 F, and winds 10 to 15 mph. Two dolphins crossed in front of the boat. These were lighter-gray skinned than those I see in Maryland and Virginia. Lots of white herons and a few others graced the course, along with pelicans engaged in lots of diving for fish. Deer peeked through the trees along the small islands next to the ocean.

Much of the route today was quite narrow. This necessitated constant attention, hands on the wheel, and very little opportunity to engage the autopilot. It also made passing oncoming boats rather tedious, as each boat jockeyed for position on the channel. This changed a bit after Wrightsville Beach as I proceeded through the Masonboro Sound, along Horseshoe Shoal, and across the Cape Fear River Inlet.

Two- and three-foot chop gradually became five, two of the three windshield wipers stopped working, the throttle seemed to stick, the GPS lost tracking data, and I got turned around and was two miles across the Atlantic Ocean part of the inlet before I realized my location and turned around. Finally I located the route to the Southport Marina and tied to the T-Head. After a shower in the bath house, I fixed the wipers, checked out the throttle cables, and was also able to get the shower drain running properly again after locating and cleaning a filter under the sink.

I then had a few beers and listened to the band at the

marina until almost midnight. Then back to the boat for some reading and a short-night's sleep. I've been apprising my buddy Jimmy Tawes of my progress, as I hope to visit him and his new wife, Mary, when I make it to Florida. He indicated the high winds and nasty thunderstorms are typical for this area and time of year. I asked him to keep me apprised of any developing hurricanes.

⚓ ⚓ ⚓

Sunday June 24, 2018
South Harbor Marina, Southport, NC
to Georgetown Landing Marina, Georgetown, SC
92 miles [434 total]

I departed at 7am for what turned out to be another long day of cruising. Today's segments were a more relaxing journey through many long straight stretches of beachfront and canal front properties. I especially liked the area between Southport and North Myrtle Beach. Boaters should be wary of a narrow stretch called "The Rock Pile." Next was a long stretch of more than thirty miles on the Waccamaw River. This took many rounded turns, becoming progressively wider and deeper the rest of the route into Georgetown SC.

After securing the boat to the main bulkhead at the marina I walked out of the marina and dined at a Taco Bell for a break from the canned food. I am especially exhausted after the late night last evening and today's 12 hours of cruising. 173 miles of SC remain before I head into Georgia's Savannah River. Weather, bridge delays, no-wake zones, and grounding notwithstanding, I may make Georgia by Tuesday evening.

⚓ ⚓ ⚓

Monday June 25, 2018
Georgetown Landing Marina, Georgetown, SC
to Charleston, SC
73 miles [507 total]

Refueled and departed Georgetown at 8:45 am. I filled the tanks with 184 gallons. The port side gauge read ¼, while the starboard fuel gauge is pegged at full all the time. The fuel gauge stick read empty- but I may not have wiggled it to the bottom of the tanks. The two fuel tanks are specified at 120 gallons each. So ¼ full total is 60 gallons. 60 plus 184 is about 240- so it seems the port side gauge is a good indicator.

I filled the tanks prior to departure. The trip thus far

was 432 miles. So 432 mi/184 gallons is 2.35 mi/gal. Traveling at an average of 7 nm/hr., this equates to about 3 gal/hr. I have been running most of the trip at 2000 rpm. This is about what I expected regarding these calculations. For example, traveling 1000 miles takes 143 hours and 429 gallons of diesel.

I saw a sign on the docks instructing not to feed the alligators. I asked if they see many by the marina and was told they just shot an eleven-footer. Apparently it was making the marina diver nervous. There were lots of tarpon jumping right next to the boat. While I've been watching for gators, I have yet to see one.

The weather forecast for the day was about the same as it was every day of the trip thus far: hot and humid, with chance of afternoon showers and possibly violent thunderstorms. I left the Georgetown dock with 70% humidity and 82 F. The late- afternoon strong winds continue making anchoring out a challenge.

A storm hit the area just as I passed through Charleston. While I had planned to push on, the storm convinced me to stop. I tied up to a bulkhead at a marine yard across from some stranded fishermen. The marine forecast detailed severe thunderstorms all around the area, with a special storm alert including potentially damaging winds.

⚓ ⚓ ⚓

Tuesday June 26, 2018

Charleston, SC bulkhead
to Ladys Island Marina, Beaufort, SC
60 miles [567 total]

I decided to leave before daybreak, but had trouble pulling away from the dock. I released the bow, planning to hold the boat against the bulkhead while I went to the stern, released the stern line, and pushed off. Wind pushed the bow out so fast I could not hold the boat against the bulkhead. I had to jump in the boat and cut the stern line with a Bowie knife, as the dinghy caught a piling and pulled out the bracket. Another swim platform repair! I secured the dinghy with a variety of ropes and headed south.

Since I wanted to repair the dinghy before going too far, I took a slip (bulkhead) 60 miles south in Beaufort at the Ladys Island Marina, arriving at 1 pm. This gave me time to walk to a hardware store to buy the clamps I would need, return to the boat, cut in the broken teak swim platform decking, mix and apply several batches of epoxy, clamp and screw the platform and reseat the dinghy. Stronger than before!

But while working with my arms under water for several hours to reattach the underwater support bracket, I could not stop thinking about gators. A guy walked by and told me there's one living at the marina, and they found eggs- indicating probably more than one gator was available to come take a bite on my arms. I was relieved when the job was finished! I celebrated my repair at a nice restaurant next to the marina called Dockside. Lots of interesting people hang around these places, including an author named Wayne Stinnett. I happened to have just read the first in his series of South Florida and Caribbean novels.

I look forward to what lies ahead! It is 39 miles to Georgia and 174 miles to Florida. Depending on how much time I buy going south, I will have more time for interesting stops on the way back.

⚓ ⚓ ⚓

Wednesday June 27, 2018
Ladys Island Marina, Beaufort, SC
to Kilkenny Marina, Richmond Hill, GA
78 miles [645 total]

Left Beaufort at 8am after a few additional reinforcing screws on the swim deck repair. The temperature was 83 F. Traveling the Beaufort River I passed Parris Island, where I took some Army training courses years ago. I then crossed the Chechessee River to Dolphin Head, passing Hilton Head Island into the Calibogue Sound. A short stretch of the Cooper River took me into the New River. Pelicons flew by in a V formation, like a flock of geese. Then the Fields Cut crossed the Savannah River just below the state line.

Lots of twists and turns and some narrow cuts brought me into the Wilmington River past the Isle of Hope. Some more short cuts and stretches of rivers took me down the Vernon River. At this point the showers and violent thunderstorms began in earnest and it was tough going. The windows kept fogging up, requiring constant wiping to maintain visibility. A very narrow passage called Hell Gate proved quite challenging, as a tug pushing a barge came out my entranceway and squeezed me nearly to the shallow water.

I then crossed the Little Ogeechee and Ogeechee Rivers, down the Florida Passage to Bear River. The storms continued, with severe lightning striking all around me. After a few more miles I detoured two miles up Kilkenny Creek to the Kilkenny Marina in Richmond Hill, GA. This was a classic southern operation. Huge mossy oaks lined the short walk to Marker 7 restaurant, where I enjoyed a folk guitarist and a great meal of buffalo shrimp, fried chicken, sweet potatoes, string beans, tomato/jalapeno pepper sauce, and key lime pie. No canned soup this evening!

While I sat on a screened deck waiting for dinner, an object "floated by" in the creek. On second glance, it was clear this was an alligator. A patron estimated it at about five feet based on the size of the head protruding from the water. I've been watching for gators and now finally saw one. I was told I will not usually see them in the Intracoastal, as the water is too salty there.

The Florida border is 96 miles at MM 710! At MM 987 I will turn up the St. Lucie River at about MM 987 (373 miles from here.) It is then 134 miles to the Gulf Coast. I must soon begin studying the charts for that phase of the trip over to the Gulf of Mexico Intracoastal.

⚓ ⚓ ⚓

Thursday June 28, 2018
Kilkenny Marina, Richmond Hill, GA
to Brunswick Landing Marina, Brunswick, GA
71 miles [716 total]

After departing at 6:45 in perfect 79 F weather the forecast for afternoon showers came over the marine radio. Since my cell phone died, I decided to take a slip in Brunswick, where there's a Verizon store nearby. My flip phone cost me $7 just eight months ago, but today their cheapest phone was $120. I was stuck and needed a phone. So I bought the "low-end" flip phone. I took a cab to the store and returned with the new phone and some groceries from Target as well.

Today's 70-mile cruise involved hours of narrow channels and much less open water and autopilot opportunities. It's now 30 miles to the Florida border. I am pleased with the progress and with fabulous sightseeing every part of the cruise! For now, the SWAMP FOX really has become my home. I planned to do a few hours of various little projects after the day's cruising. But it has not been dry enough when I get to the docks! While the weather was nice overall thus far, there have been lots of rain showers.

⚓ ⚓ ⚓

Friday June 29, 2018
Brunswick Landing Marina, Brunswick, GA
to Beach Marina, Jacksonville Beach, Florida
71 miles [787 total]

I departed Brunswick Landing Marina at 8:20 am, after pumping out, filling the fresh water tank, and checking the oil. For the trip back I must plan for the 2 ½- foot low tide in Jekyll Creek. The tide rose until 10:30 today so I was lucky. The temperature was 82F and, according to the National Weather Service, "Tropical cyclone production not expected in the next five days." The skies cleared significantly; and I passed into Florida on flat calm water, and cooler breezes than the past few days.

After a fair amount of meandering around, I passed through Fernandina Beach from Georgia into Florida. I hit bottom several times between MM 730 and 740- another area to pass at high tide. This will require planning and possibly loss of time. Thus far I've been lucky and was able to back the boat off the sand bars where I ran aground. I did this mostly with a bit of reverse and the bow thruster.

After a very stressful stretch of shallow water, I pulled into the marina in Jacksonville Beach, just as a six-piece band was starting to play at the Tiki Bar. I ate a sandwich and listened to the band for an hour. Then it was back to the boat for some reading and to rest up for another long day of cruising.

Saturday June 30, 2018
Beach Marina, Jacksonville Beach, Florida
to Halifax Harbor Marina, Daytona Beach, Florida
84 miles [871 total]

I left at 7am in 78F 87% weather. The day began with some nice easy straight open fairways. These were a welcome respite from yesterday's meandering shallows. The tides range about five feet here! Palm trees and tall pines line my starboard-side shore line, while great-looking homes line Roscoe Blvd. to the port side.

In addition to the usual dolphin displays and birds- two pink birds flew by. They were smaller than the Flamingos I've seen in the past. With the concentration required to stay in the channels and keep the boat on course, there's not a lot of time for birding or extended gazing at the shorelines. I spend a lot of time with my hand on the wheel, fine tuning the boat's course through the waterway.

A short walk from the marina found me in an Irish Pub enjoying the prime rib special, followed by a Fuente "best seller" cigar for the walk back. While working for a year in Mexico I would enjoy Cuban cigars after dinner with colleagues. I slept soundly and was up early and ready for another great cruising day.

⚓ ⚓ ⚓

Sunday July 1, 2018
Halifax Harbor Marina, Daytona Beach, Florida
to Cocoa Village Marina, Cocoa, Florida
66 miles [937 total]

I left the docks at 7:15am under clear skies, 79F and 89%. Lots of manatee zones requiring "no wake" and very slow speeds made the morning progress less than I'd hoped. I did see a few humps of the large beasts as I cruised through the designated zones. After cruising through Mosquito Lagoon I entered what turned out to be a very long stretch of the Indian River that extended into much of Monday's cruise.

While I hoped to travel more than 66 miles, I was ready to call it a day when I arrived at Cocoa Beach. I have been pushing hard to make the miles so I have more reserve time for the trip back. I'm also looking forward to visiting my old friend Jim Tawes and his new wife Mary in Saint James City, near the Gulf side exit of the Okeechobee canal route.

I hoped to locate better charts for the upcoming Okeechobee segment. So I took a bus across the bridge to a West marine store the marina manager assured me would be open. But I believe he forgot it was Sunday and they close at 5 pm. So I took the bus back over the bridge, found an open-air pizza joint, and barely managed to stay awake long enough to eat my food. I returned to the boat for a good sleep.

⚓ ⚓ ⚓

Monday July 2, 2018
Cocoa Village Marina, Cocoa, Florida
to Sailfish Marina of Stuart, Stuart, Florida
90 miles [1027 total]

Having rested well, I departed the marina at 6 am sharp. I left under a promising 82F 78%, clear skies, and hoping to make it to the entrance to the Okeechobee segment. At 6:15 am I heard a loud unusual bang in the engine room. The water temperature gauge shot way up, but the oil pressure was good. Steam rose from the engine as I lifted the hatch to examine the problem. It turned out the water hose to the engine came unclamped and I lost most of my coolant (mostly water) - hence the forward bilge pump running.

I refilled the radiator, clamped the hose, made a note to double clamp the hose as soon as possible, and was under way again in about 30 minutes. I realized how fortunate I've been to make it this far without too many difficulties.

A holdup for extensive repairs would detract greatly from the trip.

I react to any strange noises while operating the boat. A series of strange cracking slaps did not correlate to the wave action. Suddenly I glanced out the starboard window to see a dolphin racing alongside the boat and leaping out of the water, parallel to the boat. This occurred a dozen times; and there were also three or four series of these events during the next few hours. This was something I had not seen up to this point in the trip.

⚓ ⚓ ⚓

Tuesday July 3, 2018
Sailfish Marina of Stuart, Stuart, Florida
to Roland Martin's Marina and Resort, Clewiston, FLA
75 miles [1102 total]

I departed Stuart at 6:30 AM, MM 0 on the Okeechobee Waterway, starting up the St. Lucie River. After opening the Roosevelt Bridge I arrived at the St. Lucie Canal at 8am. This led to the St. Lucie Lock, which took the boat up 13 feet! Lock hands drop lines to the boat, and the boaters take up slack as the water level rises. The entire process- waiting for the gates to open, locking up and out, took about 90 minutes.

After transport through the Port Mayaca lock and out onto Lake Okeechobee I decided to take the inside route along the perimeter of the lake- rather than crossing directly across the lake. Two reasons justified this decision. First is the coral outcropping partway across the lake route, where many boaters damage props. The second reason for the inside route today was the forecast for thunderstorms. Lightning delayed the opening of a hand-operated swivel bridge but I finally made it to my target destination of Clewiston.

A small dead gator floated near the boat as I tied up. After some fish tacos at the waterside Tiki bar I called it a night. The canal here is quite narrow and I will have to back out to a turning basin past a sailboat and a sport fisher about fifty yards in the morning- unless the other boats leave before me around daybreak. Higher chances of rain are in the forecast for the area for the next several days- so I may as well get an early start tomorrow.

Despite tomorrow's weather I hope to make it to Fort Myers or Cape Coral tomorrow. Then it will be a shorter day over to Saint James City to visit Jim and Mary Tawes. Shortly into the day tomorrow the lakeside route takes me through the Moore Haven Lock into the Caloosahatchee Canal and then River to Fort Myers and Cape Coral. I hope to make it to Jim's by Thursday, where the plan is to catch up, tour the area by car, and take a few days to rest up before turning around and heading north. There are some storms now brewing.

⚓ ⚓ ⚓

Wednesday July 4, 2018
Roland Martin's Marina and Resort, Clewiston, FLA
to City of Fort Myers Yacht Basin, Fort Myers, Florida
70 miles [1172 total]

I set the alarm for 5:30, walked upstairs from the stateroom, and immediately heard a knock on the side of the boat. It was the dock master, asking me if I was the one who wanted fuel (no). He then said I may need to move to let a boat in for fuel. He was dressed in all red, white, and blue patriotic garbs. I told him OK, and then didn't hear from him again.

I backed out of the slip at 6 am (76F/89%) and proceeded west along the lake into a tunnel of ominous storm clouds, accompanied by thunder and lightning in the vicinity. A contentious air filled the early hour as a cat and a heron fought over several live bait fish thrown onto the walkway from the bait store as it opened. It appeared brighter on the forward horizon. It seemed I could run out from under the bad weather, which is what happened for the rest of the day's cruising.

This brought to mind one June afternoon when I was motoring my previous boat *OLD DAD* from the Northeast River to Saint Michaels, MD for the annual Father's Day weekend Antique and Classic Boat Show. There was a small-craft advisory for the Chesapeake, but *OLD DAD* was hardly a small craft. And I always loved that show and was determined to get there. I had assembled a canopy out over the aft deck, with wood slats sewn into the canvas, and the leading edge attached to the salon cabin.

By the time I reached the Chester River leading to the Kent Narrows the sky was very black behind me for a 180-degree field of view. I ran full-out to beat the storm. But the clouds came up over me and I was in the middle of the worst storm I ever rode out in a boat. I donned my life jacket and decided, if the boat went down, I would swim for the shore near Rock Hall. I lost all visibility and the roaring winds tossed the awning slats around like toothpicks. I feared the slats would fly through the rear windows as I heard shredding sounds of tearing canvas. The tearing sounds would simply not quit.

Just as I feared the worst, the rains and the storm over top of me had a calming effect on the water, and my visibility suddenly extended out about 20 yards. I knew then I would make it to the boat show. But I cast a fearful glance aft and discovered the awning had been torn to shreds. None of the slats left the boat, and I wrapped up the whole mess and continued to the Kent Narrows. What a disappointment, as I lost points in the judging the previous year because I did not have the awning installed.

When I arrived the dock hands were not only amazed I came through the storm, but they also felt bad about the awning- knowing why I had installed it ahead of time. So while it's tempting to hope to drive out from under bad weather, I know the weather can just as easily drive over the boat.

I rounded Liberty Point at 7am on the 4th of July. Occasional pink or white wildflowers scattered the marsh leading to the More Haven Lock, which dropped me down three feet into the Caloosahatchee Canal. The canal crossed Lake Hicpochee and continued on to the Caloosahatchee River. By now it was clear I had escaped the dark clouds of the early morning.

The shore line became denser and even more tropical looking as Ortona Lock dropped me another 8 feet. Cattle and some horses now grazed on grassy shorelines, just as an alligator swam in front of the boat and dove as I got close. The Franklin Lock dropped another 18 inches and

I proceeded into the Fort Myers Yacht Basin. This put me in easy reach of tomorrow's destination to see Jim and his wife Mary.

I checked in to the marina and set up my computer to grade papers and assignments for my online class. It rained into the evening; and the forecast is a bit bleak for tomorrow. I hope to cruise to Jim's by about noon and beat the storms for tomorrow. I've routed my course into Jim's neighborhood in Saint James City on Pine Island. The entrance from the waterway may be a bit tricky, but all this rain may make the entrance a bit more forgiving in depth.

⚓ ⚓ ⚓

Thursday July 5, 2018
City of Fort Myers Yacht Basin, Fort Myers, Florida
to Jim and Mary Tawe's home, Saint James City, Florida
22 miles [1194 total]

After a loud and rainy evening on the docks in Fort Myers, along with a spectacular fireworks display, I departed on the final leg to visit my friends on Pine Island. Despite my careful study of the charts, I made a wrong turn navigating my way into the Saint James City canals. I ran aground and could not get myself off the sandbar. I tried a few tricks with the anchor but was unable to move the boat. High tide (up a foot!) was not for another six hours so I called BoatUS, with whom I subscribe for unlimited towing.

The SeaTow boat showed up and was able to pull me off the sand bar in short order. I then followed him in the correct approach to the island and was tied up at Jim's piers twenty minutes later. While good charts provide necessary guidance, one storm can change the passage through a sandbar. My charts were accurate at the time they were printed. This ordeal was accompanied by some difficulties receiving a delivery I had scheduled to Jim's of a marine cable to 110-volt plug adapter I needed to plug in the boat- most desired for cooler sleeping in the air-conditioning. So the first night was a hot one. But it sure was great to catch up with my very good friends, Jim and Mary.

⚓ ⚓ ⚓

Friday July 6-12, 2018
Jim and Mary Tawe's home, Saint James City, Florida

Jim and Mary have set up a shop in their home to produce special rock specimens and jewelry. It's all very artistic and crafty- and beyond my knowledge, but quite interesting. Lapidary is the correct term for those who create from stones. Jim was always an entrepreneur through his career. His businesses included campgrounds, a hotel, drive-through beverage store, hardware store and lumber yard, and real estate. He is a scholar, well-read, and graduate of Washington College. Nothing fazes Mary; and she is a great complement to Jim's eclectic interests and knowledge.

Lower Pine Island sits across the water from Sanibel Island and Captiva, famous for some of the world's nicest beaches and Gulf Coast living. The Saint James City area is far less crowded than nearby Cape Coral and Fort Myers. A bicycle path runs the length of Pine Island. While the area is probably much more active during the winter, it is a very desirable place to live. We found a number of quaint restaurants and Tiki Bars in the Saint James City area- several within walking distance of the boat. It's been a great visit, despite Jim's struggles in recovering from some recent back surgery.

This has been a great rest stop. I slept twelve hours the other night. During these days I'm enjoying numerous mini-tours about the area, catching up with my friends, grading midterm exams in my online course, and doing some general cosmetic and maintenance items on the boat.

The days have passed quickly. While unexplored Florida Keys, Everglades, Bahamas, and beyond all represent the logical progression of my extended cruise, those will have to wait for the next phase of my boating adventures.

I've cruised 1,187 miles since casting off at the Cape Charles, VA Yacht Center 18 days ago. The return trip will be a continuing adventure. Jim and Mary toured the area with me in their car, showing me how wonderful an area they chose for their retirement. They also took me to their friend's home on Pine Island to see the T-Rex he's assembling from fragments found in North Dakota. Tomorrow, Thursday July 12, represents the one-week mark for my visit. It's time to move on and head back to the Chesapeake Bay.

I've read many books by a local fiction author named Randy Wayne White, whose protagonist Doc Ford lives on Sanibel Island. We toured Sanibel and adjoining Captiva Islands, and then dined at the famous Doc Ford's Rum Bar and Grill on Sanibel. I presented Jim with the first two of White's novels as part of thanking him and Mary for their hospitality during my stay.

Thursday July 12, 2018
Jim and Mary Tawe's home, Saint James City, Florida
to City Dock, La Belle, Florida
54 miles [1248 total]

I am up at 5am, thinking about the trip ahead. I plan about 55 miles today, as I'll leave near the high tide close to noon. Then tomorrow I'll cross the lake and back over to the east coast of Florida. I hope to plan ahead accurately so as to avoid the very shallow waters I encountered on portions of the trip down. Running aground even temporarily is a stressful event, as prop damage represents huge expense and schedule disruption.

I left Jim's place before noon, to catch the high tide out. This was no problem, as I had five to six feet right out his canal. I made it 54 miles before the thunderstorms kicked in, which took me right to the city dock in La Belle. The great thing about the La Belle dock was the price: free!

Two guys came in on two sailboats from Galveston, Texas. They were there to take a group of kids out on their boats and up the river to hunt for fossils. Le Belle looked like a nice town, but the thunder storm raged on through the night. So I stayed in the boat, graded some papers, read, and went to sleep.

⚓ ⚓ ⚓

Friday July 13, 2018

City Dock, La Belle, Florida
to Indian Town Marina, Indian Town, Florida
85 miles [1333 total]

I rolled out at 6:45 with an immediate bridge opening. During the first hour I spotted several large gators swimming up ahead of the boat. When I got to within 10 yards they made noisy splashes and rolled under the surface. I saw one resurface fairly quickly. This was in 15 to 20 feet of water depth. This area runs across the top parts of the Everglades and is named "Glade Land."

There was a heavy morning mist over very calm waters as I headed eastward on the waterway. Several locks including the eight-foot lift at Ortona Lock, took me up to the Lake level. As I waited for the lock to fill at Ortona a colorful dragonfly perched on top of my antenna. It had a bright orange body, while several others were bright yellow. This reminded me of the numerous dragonflies that visited my old Koi pond in Maryland. I was told they kept the mosquitos at bay, which seemed to be the case.

I covered 14 miles in the first two hours, with a 45-minute delay at the Ortona Lock. There it took fifteen minutes to get a response from the grumpy bridge tender, who told me he was busy. It was another beautiful clear day. I have yet to start the day in a storm, except for the cloud tunnel storm I drove out from under one morning in Clewiston. And while there were black clouds behind me today as I exited the Lake, it looked like a clear evening in Indian Town.

The last part of the trip was suspenseful. After driving 11 hours and 15 minutes, I made it to the Port Mayaca Lock out of Lake Okeechobee with just minutes to spare. I was the last transit of the day, as the locks close at 5 pm. A little luck never hurt anyone!

This evening I'll try the new solar shower I hang off the boom, as the first one only lasted two weeks. I had another delivered to Jim's house along with a water heater wand that plugs into my 12-volt socket at the helm. That way I don't need to use the microwave to heat water for my instant coffee. I am told there are also 12-volt coffee makers available. Maybe another time!

Tomorrow it will be 30 miles back to the Intracoastal Waterway. I'll shoot for either Ft. Pierce (50 miles total) or Vero Beach (65 miles total) for the day. Then I must plan for the areas where I need a higher tide than what I struggled through coming down. I can take a bit longer getting home and enjoy some new places.

⚓ ⚓ ⚓

Saturday July 14, 2018
Indian Town Marina, Indian Town, Florida
to Suntex Marina (Loggerhead) Vero Beach, Florida
68 miles [1401 total]

As I was leaving Indian Town at 7am (77F/78%) and photographing a rather large alligator near the boat a huge snake swam by about ten yards away. It had wide bands of black and yellow, head about a foot out of the water, diameter perhaps 4 or 5 inches, length ten or twelve feet, large flat head, swimming quickly toward the exit channel from the marina. Following just behind this snake was the tail of a Manatee! I was not able to get a good photo of the snake.

Anxious to determine what type of snake this was, I called the marina. They seemed disinterested and told me it "was just a snake." Indeed. The closest I could match is a Florida banded water snake, of which there are several varieties. After further consideration, I realized this was not a species native to Florida and what I observed was a Burmese Python. The tail was exactly that of a manatee. I don't know why the snake would have been directly over top of a manatee- but that's what I saw.

After long straight stretches of the St. Lucie Canal to the St. Lucie Lock, in flat calm water, no breeze except my own blowing my Chesapeake Bay Grand Bank Owners Association burgee on the small bow mast, it was time to head north up the Florida coast. After harrowing boat traffic through Ft. Pierce I located a very nice marina in Vero Beach- with a pool!

I pumped out, refueled, and relaxed in the pool until dark. I decided to take a rest day and stay at this marina an extra night. That will allow me to catch up on my online course, plan the next few days up the coast, walk to the grocery store, read, write, and relax.

I'm very pleased with how I am able to keep up with my graduate course teaching during the cruise using the GlocalMe device and internet at some of the marinas with decent service. I enjoy my balance of high school and graduate teaching, along with some SAT courses I teach at the local community college. Years ago I taught seven years at Penn State University and at a private liberal arts college for a few years. This experience was part of the reason I was motivated to develop a high school teaching career. I love the opportunity to teach and shape young minds.

I am also under contract with my technical book publisher (Taylor and Francis/CRC) to complete my work on mild traumatic brain injury. This is on the slate for the fall, along with adjusting to my new school in Salisbury MD. In parallel this fall, I plan to start writing fiction- a long-time goal I've prepared for over the years. This trip has allowed me to plan and place perspective on my paths forward. I am convinced I'd like to effect a retirement transition in Florida.

There is a waterfront trailer near Jim and Mary for sale. Today I plan to make an offer for that little home. What a great staging area for future cruising adventures! I would keep my small "go fast" boat at the dock and SWAMP FOX at one of several marinas just up the road in Pine Island, St. James City.

⚓ ⚓ ⚓

Sunday July 15, 2018
Suntex Marina (Loggerhead) Vero Beach, Florida
Rest Day!

I caught up on some minor cosmetic and maintenance items on the boat, then took a bicycle ride into a small shopping mall for some groceries and to loosen up after all the sitting and standing at the helm. After a day that went as planned, including lots of time in the pool, it's time to look at possible stopping points for tomorrow. Cocoa

Beach is 50+ miles; and I noticed an interesting-looking place on the way down called Caribbean Jack's Marina. Indian Harbor Beach is also a possibility and not as far. My return trip can now involve a bit more daytime/afternoon leisure.

I contacted the seller of the trailer and offered him his asking price. But he said he is in negotiation with another person and may be getting an offer. So I made mine good until Friday at 5 pm and asked him to let me know. Annoyingly, the guy said he may raise his price to me depending how his negotiations go!? He says he's a realtor. Oh well- probably not my realtor.

⚓ ⚓ ⚓

Monday July 16, 2018
Suntex Marina (Loggerhead) Vero Beach, Florida
to Titusville Municipal Marina, Titusville, Florida
71 miles [1472 total]

Left Vero Beach at 6:20 am under clear skies, 77F/90%. The scenery was incredibly lush along the Pelican Bay Wildlife Refuge. I'm now running at 1800 rpm, as the speed difference is minimal, but the fuel consumption significantly less. As the sun popped up over the ocean on my starboard side I was reminded of early mornings on Canadian Lakes with my father. We usually made it to Quebec or Ontario for a week or so each summer while I was growing up. Those were very memorable trips as well.

It was a very peaceful morning. An hour and twenty minutes elapsed before I passed a boat. A pelican decided to play "chicken" with me- waiting until I was nearly upon it to fly off the water- and then circling 360 degrees around the boat, acting like it wanted to land on the boat. I passed Merritt Island, 92F/55%, as the Cocoa Beach Bridge came into view far in the distance.

I noticed an interesting arrangement of painted wooden deck chairs at several houses. Red, blue, orange, purple, yellow, green, etc. colors adorned porches and decks. What was unusual was the alignment of the chairs. They were arranged in the color order of the visible light spectrum: ROYGBIV. Beyond coincidence, it was interesting so many people were aware of this!

I walked to a brew pub in town, had a Cuban Sandwich- one of my favorites- and talked with a guy who is restoring a Grand Banks 36. He seemed amazed at my production number- 32-194. The marina squeezed me into a tight slip, but local liveaboards helped guide me in.

⚓ ⚓ ⚓

Tuesday July 17, 2018
Titusville Municipal Marina, Titusville, Florida
to Adventure Yacht Harbor, Wilber-by-the-Sea, Florida
41 miles [1513 total]

I departed Titusville at 7:15 am, 84F. The first section today was a broad stretch of the Indian River along the Merrit Island Wildlife Refuge. In a through-canal to Mosquito Bay, as I proceeded very slowly in the no-wake zone, I hit a manatee. Despite my slow speed, the impact was tremendous. It rocked the boat from the slightly port-side impact. I was very glad to see the manatee swim up behind the boat, tail up and seemingly fine. Clearly, the no-wake zones protect both manatee and boater!

Following this I traveled a long stretch of no-wake zone on the North Indian River, traveling at 1400 rpm and seven knots. It was flat, calm, with no wind. By 1:30 I arrived at Wilbur-by-the-Sea, just below Jacksonville. The marina had a great Tiki Bar right on the water, where I had a great lunch, followed by a long walk on the beach. A storm shower hit during the walk and I took a cab back to the marina.

⚓ ⚓ ⚓

Wednesday July 18, 2018
Adventure Yacht Harbor, Wilber-by-the-Sea, Florida
to St. Augustine Municipal Harbor, St. Augustine, Florida
59 miles [1572 total]

I departed 6:45 am, 87F, with a half dozen bridges to start the day, heading up the Halifax River and Creek. Only one required opening. When vertical clearance is 22- to 27-feet, a common range, I err on the side of caution:

"Main Street Bridge, over. ….This is motor vessel SWAMP FOX traveling northbound. Request an opening…SWAMP FOX all clear, thank you very much."

By two pm a major storm hit me. It was another fog-on-the-windows, very poor visibility, keep-an-eye-on-the-radar type storms. Fortunately, it ended after about 30 minutes. These storms have been tough to predict and usually threaten many afternoons, and with varying intensities.

I passed a number of dogs watching me from their docks. They have been most pleasant- and rarely bark. Maybe they're too hot to get all worked up. I arrived in St. Augustine by 3pm, refueled, and took a slip.

The pedestrian walkway runs parallel to the waterfront of St. Augustine. Here I listened to a country singer/guitarist, an Irish folk singer, a jazz trio, an acoustic reggae singer, and a classic rock and roll band. After enjoying an evening in a variety of establishments I called it a night and was back on the boat by midnight. One highlight of the evening was the discovery that seven of us in the vicinity of the bar, including the guitarist, were named Mark. I'm pretty sure they weren't kidding.

⚓ ⚓ ⚓

Thursday July 19, 2018
St. Augustine Municipal Harbor, St. Augustine, Florida
to Beach Marine, Jacksonville Beach, Florida
31 miles [1603 total]

The weather looked bad as I left the marina- and a big storm hit just after I cleared the French Cape Inlet. Rain continued through much of the cruise, but I somehow avoided the edge of a major storm just out to sea. Ominous black storm clouds followed me into Jacksonville.

I traveled through the "northern right whale critical habitat." I did not notice this on the way down. But it would confirm my sighting of what appeared to be whales. I arrived at Beach Marine by 3:30 after four hours of crusing.

⚓ ⚓ ⚓

Friday July 20, 2018
Beach Marine, Jacksonville Beach, Florida
to Fernandina Harbor Marina, Fernandina Beach, Florida
30 miles [1633 total]

Yesterday was a short day, as I want to cruise MM 740 to 730 at close to high tide. This was an area of many shallow spots on my way down. There is another such short stretch in lower Georgia, so I plan three or four short runs in order to hit these sections near high tides. The cruising-time high tides are at 4:11 pm, 5:08 pm, and 5:15 am the next three days, starting today.

So I plan to depart early afternoon today. During a session in the laundromat this morning it started to rain hard. But bluer brighter skies are merging as I write this closer to noon. I spent three hours this morning on my special internet connection, grading student discussions, projects, and papers. I was also able to catch up on some emails and other school correspondence. My new school added me to their web page, so everything looks good there.

Prior to departing I smelled a "hot electrical" smell in the head, which turned out to be a blown GFI outlet. I shut off that part of the AC circuitry and will replace the breaker when I can find one at a future stop. The electrical system on SWAMP FOX is nicely done with lots of labeling, redundancy, and logic. I was not using the bathroom outlet anyway, and usually had it disabled for my inside showers.

Light rain fell most of the way today. I left the marina at 11:30 and arrived at Fernandina in four hours. High tide made the shallow stretch much easier, with just a few noticeable low depths.

⚓ ⚓ ⚓

Saturday July 21, 2018
Fernandina Harbor Marina, Fernandina Beach, Florida
to Jekyll Harbor Marina, Jekyll Island, Georgia
32 miles [1665 total]

Fernandina is a nice town- sort of a small version of St. Augustine. I dined at a nice Mexican restaurant, listened to two bands at two pubs, and returned to the boat. The marina has a serious problem where, at low tide, only a few slips do not turn into mud! They gave me what they said was their deepest slip on a T-head. A gentleman from the marina office held my bow and allowed the strong current to turn me around for departure, as there was not enough deep water to turn around at the dock.

I made it in four hours to Jekyll Island, just as very strong winds and rain greeted me at the dock. Today I crossed into Georgia. For the first stretch of the ICW the markers switched from green right to red right- then back again at the Navy station at King's Bay. A broad expanse of the Cumberland River took me into the mouth of the ocean and back in in order to hit sufficient channel depth. This was a bit thought provoking, as strange dark storm clouds gathered overhead.

Tomorrow I planned to reserve a dock space at the Two Way Fish Camp which is 3 miles off the ICW MM 664. This is so I can cross Jekyll Creek just ahead, which is only two and a half feet at low tide. High tide tomorrow is at 4:27 am and 5:13 pm. Leaving at 4 pm would get me to the Fish Camp by dark. But this is just 22 miles. The problem is, they will not take a reservation! They have a spot open now but I am to call tomorrow afternoon to see if it's still available.

Plan B is to leave MM 685 at daylight (6 am), cross Jekyll Creek (MM 685 to 680), and also cross Little Mud River (MM 655 to 650) closer to the high tide at 5:13 pm- perhaps around 2 pm by traveling slower in the interim stretch. Kilkenny Marina is at MM 614 +2. Therefore from about 2:30 pm to dark I will need to cover 48 miles. I will likely start up the Little Mud River as early as possible and wait for more tide if I hit bottom. Tomorrow will be a tricky day.

At the moment I am pushed up against a long pier with boats in front and behind me. If there's still wind like what is blowing right now it will be tough getting away from the pier. So I will get up at 5 am and evaluate all over again. Lots of variables!

⚓ ⚓ ⚓

Sunday July 22, 2018
Jekyll Harbor Marina, Jekyll Island, Georgia
to Two-Way Fish Camp, Duck, Georgia
28 miles [1693 total]

With the help of a dock hand I tied off the bow, nudged the boat in forward with the wheel turned all right, and pushed the stern out into the current- then released the bow line and backed away from the pier. This was at 7:30 am (95F). I hit one low spot on Jekyll Creek but made it through. Because of the timing I only traveled across the St. Simons Sound, up the Mackay River, and three miles up the South Altamaha River to the Two-Way Fish Camp. After four hours I tied off at a T Head into wind and strong current. The storms missed me today but I did not reciprocate!

It's interesting how, when crossing a sound, or cruising a mile or two into the ocean, a different rhythm takes over. The more random chop takes on the harmonic rhythm of the ocean, with a characteristic lapse or period between swells. This often intermixes with the effects of winds and tides to produce a very different "ocean feel" even in proximity to the high sea.

The Altamaha River is listed in the Nature Conservancy's "Last 75 Great Places." There's a half-day tour of the area for bird watching, also featuring over 1000-year old cypress trees, big alligators, Civil War lore, and more. I would like to stop by here again someday and take that tour.

Three large (eight- to ten-foot) gators floated along the dock as I walked to the office to pay for my dockage. The largest swam around all afternoon by the fish cleaning station, without luck as no fish were being cleaned today. I ate a great lunch at the little waterfront café and returned to the boat for a long nap.

My plan for the next two days is to leave tomorrow at daybreak to take advantage of the 5:18 am high tide (with an add-on time of up to two hours for this area) and clear the Little Mud River trouble spot by 8 am. Then I'll proceed on to the Kilkenny Marina for a 50-mile day. Tuesday I'll cruise 59 miles and stop somewhere in Hilton Head,

SC. This is all weather permitting as always. But I've not been slowed much by the weather.

⚓ ⚓ ⚓

Monday July 23, 2018
Two-Way Fish Camp, Duck, Georgia
to Kilkenny Marina, Richmond Hill, GA
50 miles [1743 total]

I departed Duck, Georgia's Two-Way Fish Camp about 7am (73F). I followed yesterday's trail out, with a high tide to help further assure adequate depth. A coast guard boat with a marker buoy on board and some heavy winching equipment parked right in front of me, which worried me, should anything let go and drop onto the bow of the SWAMP FOX.

I saw a gator swimming in the creek last time here-but saw none this time. It was a nice night to sit out on the stern. A steady breeze blew the entire night, and then stopped by daybreak. Off to Hilton Head!

⚓ ⚓ ⚓

Tuesday July 24, 2018
Kilkenny Marina, Richmond Hill, GA
to Shelter Cove Marina, Hilton Head, SC
58 miles [1801 total]

With the ebbing high tide I cleared through Little Mud Creek with only minor difficulties where I had to feel my way through the shallow spots. Just before I came to Little Mud Creek, nine dolphins greeted me. This felt like a good luck omen. I made it through without much trouble. The Fields Cut is tricky at its southern entrance- and on the falling half-tide. This area slowed me down due to some contact with the bottom.

Strange clouds with continual lightening threatened toward the ocean. But the weather held nicely through the day. It was a nice 58-mile day. I noted the temperature of 98F through the Isle of Hope area. Then I crossed the Savannah River into South Carolina.

I selected a very nice marina for the night, six miles up Broad Creek at Hilton Head. The two dockhands actually pumped my fuel and emptied the holding tank for me. The norm is to be handed the pumps and left to the task on my own. These seemed like great kids who knew how to work.

There were seven restaurants around the dock. I found an outdoor Tiki bar at a Mexican restaurant, ate tacos and listened to music. Tuesday night at this place features fireworks which I watched from the stern before calling it a night.

⚓ ⚓ ⚓

Wednesday July 25, 2018
Shelter Cove Marina, Hilton Head, SC
to Downtown Marina of Beaufort, SC
35 miles [1836 total]

It was an easy departure from the dock, with no wind, current, or tides. I rolled out at 6:10 am, following the markers six miles out of Broad Creek and back to the ICW. I crossed a seven-mile expanse of Port Royal Sound at 8:30am and 89 F. Once again the ocean swell cast a different feel to the cruise.

I arrived at downtown Beaufort and took the marina courtesy car to the local PaLo for groceries. After a shower and some reading and writing, I walked around the docks and discovered a boat I'd heard about and seen one picture. It is a 1929 Red Bank. My former boat OLD DAD was a Red Bank Yachtworks Motorcruiser as well. To my knowledge, these are the last two of the large Red Banks still afloat. I looked it over and took some pictures. I find these old boats fascinating, and quite interesting in their design and features. I inquired at the office, but unfortunately I'm told the owner is not around much.

⚓ ⚓ ⚓

Thursday July 26, 2018
Downtown Marina of Beaufort, SC
to St. John's Yacht Harbor, Charleston, SC
64 miles [1900 total]

I shoved off the dock in Beaufort at 6:30 am to catch the last bridge opening before rush-hour traffic- but it turned out I had sufficient clearance and did not require an opening. High tide was at 8:30, making it nice getting through the various river-connecting "cutoffs", such as the Ashepoo-Coosaw cutoff. I began the day with about nine-ty minutes of peaceful calm open water out the Coosaw River.

By noon I crossed Wadlamaw Island and proceeded into the last stretch for the day. It was now almost dead low tide, down six or seven feet in a long and meandering channel. I drove through 40 minutes of rain, arriving at 3 pm.

With my new teaching position starting in about a

month, I find myself looking forward to a new school. I anticipate good leadership and a collegial environment. In my previous employment I became accustomed to more professionalism and positive culture than I experienced in some of the public school systems. Training better teachers is not the root cause solution to much of what I observed. We need better-equipped management! While I enjoyed the insights of some of the many administrators with whom I interacted, many would benefit from some proper training. Although the old adage, "leaders are born, not trained" holds true in the education field.

I'm also looking forward to the completion and culmination of the SWAMP FOX story. This represents a major epoch in my lifetime database. I collect many boating books, including all those I can find on the ICW. I look forward to reaching many readers with this book, as it's a book I would enjoy reading. This work is also a transition to another of my goals.

I always had the desire to write fiction. From an early age, I read with ongoing analysis of how an author constructed a story, including plot, dialogue, character development, and delivery. For a good part of my life, I would pass along to my father the books I had read; and he would read them as well. Then we would discuss the books from many perspectives. My father was a brilliant man; and I miss those discussions a lot. Fortunately, I have the ability to recall conversations almost verbatim from many years ago, and can revisit interesting thoughts from my past.

My father's master's degree was in English literature. While I studied an extensive range of multidisciplinary subject matter, literature was not one of my degrees. I enjoy lifelong learning and have augmented my professional skills with academic work in numerous areas. Having done so in my current field of education with a pair of master's degrees in math education and mathematics, I feel content in my formal education and desire for knowledge through the avenues of formal learning.

⚓ ⚓ ⚓

Friday July 27, 2018
St. John's Yacht Harbor, Charleston, SC
to Harbor Walk Marina, Georgetown, SC
73 miles [1973 total]

I departed Charleston at 6:15 am. After a few hours I encountered heavy rain, lightening, and thunder, and very poor visibility. Otherwise the trip was uneventful, with the usual variety of beautiful waterfront scenery, providing plenty of time to relax, reflect, and think.

I learned some of the newer docks are wired with ground fault interrupts at the dock boxes which cause less than optimal performance of my air conditioning unit. This has happened several times on the voyage, and may require some simple rewiring of the ac circuit at some point. The ac shut down in the middle of the night, making for some hot sleeping.

Another variable I encountered at my marina stopovers is computer WIFI quality and performance. My GlocalMe MIFI data is running quite low; and it appears I need to reactivate my PayPal account to be able to purchase more data. Marinas with reliable internet are great, as I can do my schoolwork and correspondence without burning up data. On Spot WIFI service works great wherever I encounter it. I was told the company inventor/owner's boat was parked at tonight's marina; and they had just finished installing this great service.

Georgetown is a nicely developed small town with a small board walk along the shopping and restaurant district. I found a nice little Mexican restaurant and enjoyed three bands in different establishments. I also sampled one of the three ice cream parlors along the river front. I always meet interesting people along my route.

One older gentleman, balanced on the park bench, informed me as I walked by that "you can't drink all day."

I agreed as I walked past, after which he shouted to me, "unless you start in the morning!" I love a great sense of humor- if not just great humor.

I was surprised to note two instances of the name SWAMP FOX. First was a signboard for SWAMP FOX tours- History, Mystery, and Romance. - apparently guided walking tours of the historic district. I also discovered the SWAMP FOX drink- a rum concoction with orange and pineapple juice and grenadine. Also in South Carolina are SWAMP FOX movie theaters, art galleries, and entertainment centers.

Revolutionary War hero Francis Marion (aka SWAMP FOX) was born and buried in South Carolina. He fought the British occupation of South Carolina and Charleston, serving in the Continental Army and South Carolina militia. Considered the father of guerrilla warfare, his contributions are noted in the development of US Army Rangers and Special Forces such as the Green Berets. I think it's also a great name for a boat.

⚓ ⚓ ⚓

Saturday July 28, 2018
Harbor Walk Marina, Georgetown, SC
to Myrtle Beach Yacht Club, Little River, SC
58 miles [2031 total]

I departed at 7 am (82F/87%) with lightening flashing to the east. Boat traffic was quite heavy through the Myrtle Beach area. Some of the boat captains simply had no idea what a poor job they were doing driving their boats. One in particular crossed right in front of me as I was navigating a bridge opening, passing a tour boat under the adjacent fixed bridge, conducting traffic for some confused rental jet ski riders (who thanked me), and generally optimizing the safety of the transition through the heavily congested area. I gave the guy a friendly warning with my horn to be sure he saw me.

This seemed to infuriate the guy, who then drove around behind me, back in front of me, blocking several other boats in proper passing positions, and then shouting vulgarities and other nonsense at me and another boat similarly worried about the safety aspect of the guy's behavior. Some radio greetings to the errant boater- and possibly the flashing lights on a police boat moments later were all related.

But I finally made it to a very nice stopping point- the Myrtle Beach Yacht Club, where a veteran dock master assisted me into a floating dock slip. I was granted an admission to the officer's club and the marina pool, where waitresses served food and beverage poolside. Later I enjoyed a truly excellent meal at the club, followed by a walk through several adjacent marinas for some boat watching.

I have a fair amount of grading and school work to catch up on- and the internet service is great here. So I decided to sleep in and make Sunday a rest day. Maybe some of the novice and crazy weekend boaters will be back to work on a weekday as I continue cruising on Monday. Some extended storms are moving through the area right now as well- further substantiating the decision to stay an extra night.

⚓ ⚓ ⚓

Sunday July 29, 2018
Myrtle Beach Yacht Club, Little River, SC
Rest Day!

This is day 40 of my journey. Lots of rain up the eastern seaboard, including almost an inch thus far today at my marina, convinced me to make this a rest day. My plan is to catch up with my graduate students online, do some reading and writing, general maintenance issues including a windshield wiper repair, laundry, and some trip planning.

Indeed it was a relaxing day as well as a productive one. My students have been working diligently on a variety of assignments in my computer science course. The book is coming along nicely; and I'm relaxing as I make my way through the Randy Wayne White series of Doc Ford novels. White spends some of his time on Pine Island, Florida, where my friends Jim and Mary reside.

I observed numerous sea turtles along the water's edge in SC. Like manatees, turtles are protected by law. Caution is advised for boaters to avoid hitting turtles that may be swimming in the waterway. Loss of habitat as civilization continues to encroach is accompanied by excellent public awareness campaigns to protect the turtles and manatees. I am grateful I was traveling at nearly idle speed when I bumped the manatee going through a bridge canal a while back. That manatee may have been a bit shaken up, but appeared to swim away unharmed from the stern of the boat right after bouncing off the port bow. Manatees grow to ten feet and more than half a ton, so they are protected to some extent by their mass and volume.

Monday July 30, 2018
Myrtle Beach Yacht Club, Little River, SC
to Seapath Yacht Club, Wrightsville Beach, NC
64 miles [2095 total]

After an inch of rainfall overnight, it rained another hour from 6 am to 7am, when I departed. After 64 miles of long straight canals and some shoaled ocean inlets breaking up the depth readings, I arrived in Wrightsville Beach. I took the marina courtesy car to a West Marine store, where I purchased a spare wiper blade. The alternate part I installed last summer has been a little troublesome. Now I'm all set, as the forecast is for more rain tomorrow. I had nachos at Poe's Restaurant (as in Edgar Allen) and some local craft beer.

I drove through rain for five straight hours today. But fortunately the visibility was mostly good, and the lightening was in the distance. I hear other transient boaters staging their next legs north, as am I. Tentatively, I'll stop at Huggins/Dudley Islands, Oriental, Belhaven, and the Alligator River Marina the next four nights. This places me conveniently for the significant stretches of Bogue Sound, Morehead City, Pamlico River/Pungo River, Alligator River and Canal, and the decision point regarding the famous Dismal Swamp Canal. That would put me in the Chesapeake Bay early next week!

⚓ ⚓ ⚓

Tuesday July 31, 2018
Seapath Yacht Club, Wrightsville Beach, NC
to Casper's Marina, Swansboro, NC
54 miles [2149 total]

This is the last day of July! I was up at daybreak as usual, and was greeted by dark clouds, wind, and rain. I waited until 8 am, for a temporary break in the weather and called in my first of the day's four bridge openings. The lady operating the bridge cheerfully indicated it would be a minute or so until she had a break in the morning traffic.

After fifteen minutes I called her again to see what was happening- and she had fallen asleep! She was very apologetic, telling me she'd been working 14 straight hours. This was not a big deal except that it caused me to miss my opening and wait 30 minutes at the subsequent bridge. I drove through rain for several thirty-minute stretches, and finally pulled against a bulkhead in Swansboro under strong winds. I walked the small town, had some dinner, and called it a night.

I saw lots of herons today, which always remind me of herons eating my fish. Back in Pennsylvania, I dammed up part of my creek and stocked it with 15-inch rainbow trout. But they disappeared quickly. One day I happened to spot the culprit, perching on my television antenna- a great blue heron. The solution was to place hollow cylinders for the fish to hide and to excavate some deep holes where the herons could not get to the fish.

In Crisfield, MD I enjoyed sitting in the back yard by my koi pond. At the peak I had about 30 fish in the 15-foot by 10-foot pond that was over four feet deep at the center. But the herons found a way! I observed from the house herons landing on the overhead pergola, jumping down to the water's edge or to a boulder in the center of the pond, pecking the fish, grabbing them in their talons, and gulping them whole!

I tried a series of recommended solutions. First was an owl decoy- no effect. Next I hung special reflective tape designed to simulate movement when the sun reflected, thus scaring the herons away- no effect. Then I strung fishing line all around the pergola and above the pond, so that the herons would fly into the lines, get confused and stop fishing there- no luck- they actually perched on the lines, and even held them down with one foot and stepped over!

Next in the series of deterrents was a heron decoy. Herons are territorial, so when the real birds saw the decoy, they would look for another spot. This lasted perhaps twenty minutes, after which the real birds ignored the decoy. I also tried the alligator heads lurking just out of the water- simulating natural predators the herons should have wished to avoid. The herons stood on the gator heads to get a better shot at the fish!

Finally, I decided there would be only one solution. I enclosed the entire pergola with flexible nylon netting like I used in my aviaries to contain the rare and exotic birds I propagated. This worked well, as the herons simply could not get into the pond area. And from a distance the netting was not visible, so it did not detract from the aesthetic appeal of the pond area. Fortunately my prior annoyance with these birds has transformed back to enjoyment in seeing them along the water's edge.

⚓ ⚓ ⚓

Wednesday August 1, 2018
Casper's Marina, Swansboro, NC
to Oriental Marina and Inn, Oriental, NC
50 miles [2199 total]

I pushed off the Swansboro bulkhead at 6:30 am. Winds were 10-15 mph, with gusts of 20 mph. This was finally some very different weather! I traveled the Bogue

Sound for 16 miles, approaching Morehead City. By 1:30 pm I was in a slip in downtown Oriental. Just across the channel was a major shrimp operation, where numerous working trawlers came to unload their catches.

I enjoyed this stop, with a swim in the pool and a huge salad in the onsite tavern. Parked next to me was a 42-foot Grand Banks trawler the owner was taking from Galveston, Texas to Charlestown Marina, where I kept my boats for years.

⚓ ⚓ ⚓

Thursday August 2, 2018
Oriental Marina and Inn, Oriental, NC
to Belhaven Marina, Belhaven, NC
48 miles [2247 total]

I negotiated out of the Oriental harbor on Raccoon Creek at 6:30, beginning the day with 2 ½ hours on the Neuse River. The water was progressively rougher, after a nice sunrise across the six-mile expanse of the Neuse. I could not see the far shore.

I then went up a small canal to the Pungo River, where I hit a big storm and very heavy seas. I made it to the Belhaven Marina, two miles off the ICW. Belhaven is designated "The Birthplace of the Atlantic Intracoastal Waterway." This is a convenient stop for ICW travelers, with much history. The small downtown area features some great restaurants, including a lunch buffet I enjoyed as the last customer of the afternoon. The marina maintains a marine railway as an alternative to hauling out with a travel lift. There are few of these still operating. Some wooden boat heritage and local builders was the topic of conversation in the marina office.

⚓ ⚓ ⚓

Friday August 3, 2018
Belhaven Marina, Belhaven, NC
to Alligator River Marina, Columbia, NC
53 miles [2300 total]

Similar to the last few early mornings, I woke to pouring rain and thunderstorms. I waited for these to subside before pushing off at 7 am. Today's cruise included the 22-mile long Alligator Canal, feeding into the Alligator River for 21 miles. I stopped here at the Alligator Marina bulkhead, leaving four miles of the Alligator leading to the Albemarle Sound.

The winds picked up for the last hour or so, making it

quite rough. I was told the shallow depths of the Albemarle Sound cause it to be about twice as rough as the River, given the same general set of conditions. The winds tomorrow, especially in the morning, should be a bit slower than today and coming from the south.

My hope is tomorrow's winds will push astern, as I travel north and north-northwest- 20 miles across the Albemarle Sound and about 15 miles up the Pasquotank River to Elizabeth City. A call to the Dismal Swamp Canal office confirmed the canal is open and all bridges and locks are operating on published schedules. This alternate route north should be an interesting segment on Sunday.

⚓ ⚓ ⚓

Saturday August 4, 2018
Alligator River Marina, Columbia, NC
to Pelican Marina, Elizabeth City, NC
35 miles [2335 total]

I left at 6 am, close to daybreak. I hoped to get well across the Sound before any extra cross waves and combinations of tides, winds, and shallow waters created an uncomfortable crossing. I had the wind of up to 10 mph on my stern for the first hour. But there was a gradual building to very rough conflicting seas crossing the Sound to the Pasquotank River. As I proceeded up the River the conditions improved again.

I arrived at the Pelican Marina in Elizabeth City, where an older live aboard regaled me with stories of the Dismal Swamp Canal. These stories included tails of snakes dropping from the trees onto the boat deck and him throwing them off his boat with a boat hook. I enjoyed a walk around the town, several taverns, and a good meal.

⚓ ⚓ ⚓

Sunday August 5, 2018
Pelican Marina, Elizabeth City, NC
to Waterside Marina, Norfolk, VA
51 miles [2386 total]

I left Elizabeth City at 7:30 am with a bridge opening. Today's trip through the Dismal Swamp Canal included sets of bridge and lock transports before and after the 22-mile canal. My plan was to travel at rates commensurate with a South Mills Lock opening at 11 am, and a Deep Creek Lock opening at 3:30- the last of the day. Unsure of the conditions in the canal, I did not want to cut it too close and have to spend the night in the canal.

I proceeded up the ever-narrowing Pasquotank River in flat calm water. This was quite the contrast to the Albemarle Sound. My timing for the day worked out well, albeit with some significant waits for the bridge/lock openings. I believe in being early for business meetings and for bridges and locks. I was amazed through the trip by captains on the radio pleading for exceptions to opening times to accommodate their lack of timeliness- never realizing there was workforce traffic crossing those bridges on schedules comparable or greater in importance.

No snakes! I did hit submerged wood five times but with no damage to the boat. I observed a huge sign set back in the woods that read SWAMP COMMANDER. I wonder if that commander is separate from the overall swamp authority. It was a nice ride through the Canal, and looked like some interesting kayaking as well. I felt relieved that the trip was uneventful in contrast to much of the hype I encountered before the event. SWAMP FOX exited the Swamp and it was on to the busy Norfolk area and the Waterside Marina.

Monday August 6, 2018
Waterside Marina, Norfolk, VA
to Windmill Point Marina, Whitestone, VA
49 miles [2435 total]

I left MM 0 of the ICW at 6am and was very fortunate to encounter flat calm seas the first few hours as I began the trip up the Chesapeake Bay. A pleasant 5 mph breeze from the south accompanied me past the Salt Ponds inlet in Hampton. This reminded me of my trip with Nipper when we ducked a storm in this same area for two days by scurrying into the Salt Pond Inlet through huge waves.

There is of course a more "wide-open" feel to the Chesapeake in contrast to much of the ICW. The water looked greenish-blue through much greater depths than on the ICW. I set various headings from my chart book on the autopilot and enjoyed the scenario as I made a 7-hour haul up the west side of the Bay.

I continued past Mobjack Bay and the mouth of the Piankatank River to Windmill Point at the mouth of the Rappahannock River. It was 91F at noon. More importantly, a dark feeling began setting in as I realized this trip must end. Soon the fall days of school would sweep me up in a cataclysm of educational activity.

The freedom of the past months in planning and executing my long-awaited trip on the ICW was giving way to the sense of responsibilities and planning inherent in effective teaching. I feel fortunate to have created the time to take the trip, and even more blessed with the ability to have overcome all the daily challenges of running a boat on the ICW.

Windmill point had a nice pool and few people to interrupt my reading and relaxing between swims in the cooler water. I began to reminisce on all that has happened along the way, realizing again how fortunate I was to have experienced this in the midst of a second career in education. My summer graduate course turned out to be the best set of students I ever taught. The students and I enjoyed a lively discussion and examination of topics in systems engineering and computer science.

⚓ ⚓ ⚓

Tuesday August 7, 2018
Windmill Point Marina, Whitestone, VA
Rest Day!

With heavy winds in tomorrow's forecast- and much improvement for the following day- I decided this was a good day for catching up on school work, writing, reading, and some quality pool time. I also found a nice Mexican restaurant in town using the marina's courtesy car. There was a lobby in the marina office with internet, where I spent the morning prior to heading to the pool.

⚓ ⚓ ⚓

Wednesday August 8, 2018
Windmill Point Marina, Whitestone, VA
to Zahniser's Yacht Club, Solomons, MD
60 miles [2495 total]

I looked forward to today's destination on Solomon's Island, as I spent some time there last summer. It is a long run to Solomon's so I left at 6am. Winds were already at 10 to 15 mph as I crossed the wide expanse of the Potomac River at 10:30 to Point Lookout. But the winds and resultant waves gradually diminished for the remainder of the cruise.

I continued past the Naval Air Warfare Center Aircraft Division (NAWCAD) into the Patuxent River to Solomon's Island and the marina. After acquiring some supplies in the ships store I was off to a nice afternoon at the combination Tiki snack bar and pool. This was the last hurrah before tomorrow's final leg into Port of Salisbury.

⚓ ⚓ ⚓

Thursday August 9, 2018
Zahniser's Yacht Club, Solomons, MD
to Port of Salisbury, MD
28 miles [2523 total]

Well, yes! as a former teacher colleague likes to exclaim. Today is the last leg of the trip. I feel saddened. I would have liked to have gone further and longer. But the new job begins in 11 days. I have a ride set up for 2 pm Friday from my colleague Bohidar. He is already gearing up for the new year at the same school. So it is time.

I rolled out of Solomon's Island at 7:30 am. There was a small craft advisory for the afternoon- 20+ mph winds and gusts up to 35 mph- but I planned to be well up the Wicomico River by then. Winds and tide seemed to push me along, as if to rush me ahead to my final destination for the trip. It felt time to get to "what's next."

It was a long run down the bay, past Lower Hooper Island on the east shore, dodging ever more crab pots over to the mouth of the Wicomico River above Deal Island. Having never navigated the Wicomico I was surprised at the excellent depths the entire way to the end at Port of

Salisbury. This is one of the nicest rivers I've navigated. The lush green grasses on either bank of the sparsely-populated lower reaches were like a gentle welcome embrace to the SWAMP FOX as I negotiated lots of twists and turns for about 15 miles to my new marina.

I received warm greetings and expert assistance from the dock master Mike in getting me into the slip of my choice at the municipal marina Port of Salisbury. I was pleased at how undeveloped the river was, even near the end, where a fuel plant and ship building yard did not detract from the pleasant landscape. I felt strange to be tied in the slip where I plan to spend several nights per week to save on the 75-minute drive from my VA bayside home to my new school.

The advertised "free WIFI" was indeed that- but with little to no signal strength, despite my close proximity to the transmit location. I was told they are in the process of upgrading, and that the problem will be resolved by Tuesday next week. This is important, as I do not wish to keep buying data on my MIFI- especially since I often stream movies in the evening to relax.

August 10 to October 7

Port of Salisbury, MD

After returning to my bayside home in Virginia I realized the trip is over and it is time to look forward to what's ahead. Subsequent to some introductory meetings at my new school I dove into review of text books, creation of syllabi, communication with colleagues, purchase of some new clothes, and organizing my teaching materials for the new school year. I am very excited to be teaching a top-tier college preparatory high school, with a group of highly capable colleagues in a collegial environment.

I am back and forth to the boat, organizing and acclimating to the Port of Salisbury. I will stay on the boat weeknights to avoid the commute to my bayside home in Virginia. I took a few walks around Salisbury and find it a very nice developing town. Near my marina are a number of nice restaurants and pubs, library, and the campus of Salisbury University. I am right next to the Brew River restaurant and Tiki Bar, where I attended boat docking contests in the past.

SWAMP FOX is at rest and serving a new purpose as my weeknight home. Upon returning from school to the boat I often take a long walk around Salisbury, while enjoying some interesting entertainment at the waterfront establishments.

The Port of Salisbury location posed a few problems though. At or near high tide, the water came over the finger pier I used to exit and enter the boat. Some mornings I had to time my departure to the shower house and car to avoid walking through as much as a foot of water on the pier. Another problem was the large resident flock of geese, that made quite a mess on the docks, requiring daily hosing of the entire length of walking area. Internet signal was spotty or nonexistent most of the time. While I tolerated these detractions, an attempted break-in to my boat in the middle of the night motivated my move down river.

October 7 - ?

Wicomico Yacht Club, Eden, MD

Following several break-ins at the marina, a person boarded my boat while I was sleeping. I felt the boat move, heard footsteps, and looked up to see a face looking in the back door window at me. I was frightened, and yelled loudly, scaring the person back off the boat. That weekend I drove to the Wicomico Yacht Club 90 minutes by boat down river, where I secured a covered slip and a membership application.

I was approved for membership in the club, where the food is excellent, people quite friendly, and the newly built clubhouse and shower facilities A+! I practically have the place all to myself except when the club is open. I pumped out my holding tank, filled the fresh water tank, and have set up camp for the winter. Sunrise on the river and the seclusion of the slip location add to a very pleasant experience to date.

As I proceed in my first year teaching at a private college prep school my mind wanders to thoughts of future cruises, Tiki bars, southern locales, and further adventure. Perhaps a bigger boat! Retirement, writing, cruising, fishing, reading... time to cast off for the next chapters!

ANNOTATED BIBLIOGRAPHY

Alexandria Drafting Company. (2001) ADC Chesapeake Bay Chartbook Maryland and Virginia. Alexandria, VA: ADC: Alexandria Drafting Company. *This is a set of very detailed reference charts essential for planning and navigating the Bay.*

Chesapeake Bay Magazine, eds. (2017) Atlantic Coast and ICW Planning and Facilities Guide. Annapolis, MD: Chesapeake Bay Media, LLC. *This excellent compendium not only provides an ordered set of bridges, canals, locks, and marinas– it also features useful articles and planning data.*

Kettlewell, John, and Leslie Kettlewell, eds. (2012) The *Intracoastal* Waterway Chartbook Norfolk, Virginia, to Miami, Florida. Camden ME: The McGraw Hill Companies. *I was not able to find a more recent edition of this excellent Chartbook. Some of the information was a bit off, such as marker placement, location of the channels, etc. Fortunately the software on my chart plotters was only a few years old.*

Kettlewell, John, and Leslie Kettlewell, eds. (2004) The *Intracoastal* Waterway Chartbook Miami, Florida, to Mobile, Alabama. Camden ME: The McGraw Hill Companies. *I was not able to find a more recent edition of this excellent Chartbook. Some of the information was a bit off, such as marker placement, location of the channels, etc. Fortunately the software on my chart plotters was only a few years old.*

Maptech Embassy Guides, eds. (2005) Chesapeake Bay to Florida. Amesbury, MA: Maptech, Inc. *While my first edition was a bit outdated, this book provides lots of useful local knowledge and ICW data.*

Nautical Publications. (2017) United States Boating Pilot 10 *Intracoastal* Waterway. US Department of Commerce, NOAA. *"The U.S. Boating Pilots are reproductions of the official NOAA Coast Pilot with masses of other useful information added in an interactive app." I suppose one of these days I should buy a smart phone. This free app would have been quite useful.*

APPENDIX 1

Boat Survey

Tranquil Waters
MARINE SERVICES
Commercial & Recreational
Vessel Surveys

6670 Windmill Point Road
White Stone, Virginia 22578

804-435-0040   Fax 804-435-0042
Email: tranquilw@rivnet.net

CONDITION AND VALUATION SURVEY REPORT

This is to certify that the undersigned surveyor did on March 9, 2017 at the request of Mark Mentzer, attend the vessel *Sea to See* to perform a pre-purchase condition and valuation survey. The vessel was seen while underway and hauled at Atlantic Yacht Basin, located in Great Bridge, Virginia.

This report is for the exclusive use of the named requester, his underwriters, and lending institution on his behalf. It may not be transferred to any other party. The estimated value is based on a general market research with consideration given to findings. It should be used for financial and insurance purposes only.

Description of Vessel

Name	Sea to See
Description	Wooden, classic trawler motor vessel
Builder	American Marine Ltd.
Place Built	Hong Kong, China
Year	1970
Builders Hull Number	32-194
Official Number	528917
Length Overall	31 Feet 11 Inches
Beam	11 Feet 6 Inches
Draft	3 Feet 9 Inches
Displacement	17,000 lbs
Gross Tons	10
Net Tons	8
Estimated Replacement Value	$ 385,000
Suitability for Intended Service	Good

- 135 -

Appendix 2

Diesel Purchases

1. Filled the two 120-gallon tanks for departure- total approximately $800.00
2. Georgetown, SC 160 gallons $533
3. Palm Coast, FLA 162 gal $542
4. Stuart, FLA 73 gal $230
5. Vero Beach, FLA 145 gal $478
6. St. Augustine, FLA 61 gal $216
7. Hilton Head, SC 80 gal $260
8. Swansboro, NC 110 gal $296

Remaining in tank: Approx. 80 gallons at end of cruise

Total fuel consumption: 951 gallons approximately $3100

The engine meter logged 411 hours

This averages to 2.3 gallons per hour

APPENDIX 3

Marinas and Anchorages

Day 1- June 20
Coinjock Marina- Coinjock, NC
http://www.coinjockmarina.com/

Day 2- June 21
Anchored near Belhaven, NC

Day 3- June 22
Dudley's Marina- Swansboro, NC
https://www.dudleysmarinanc.com/

Day 4- June 23
South Harbour Marina- Southport, NC
http://www.southharbourmarina.com/

Day 5- June 24
Georgetown Landing Marina- Georgetown, SC
http://georgetownlandingmarina.com/

Day 6- June 25
Bulkhead south of Charleston, SC

Day 7- June 26
Lady's Island Marina- Beaufort, SC
http://www.ladysislandmarina.com/

Day 8- June 27
Kilkenny Marina-Richmond Hill, GA
no website; see FB

Day 9- June 28
Brunswick Landing Marina- Brunswick, GA
https://brunswicklandingmarina.com/

Day 10- June 29
Beach Marine- Jacksonville Beach, FLA
https://www.jaxbeachmarine.com/

Day 11- June 30
Halifax Harbor Marina- Daytona Beach, FLA
http://www.halifaxharbormarina.com/

Day 12- July 1
Cocoa Village Marina- Cocoa, FLA
http://www.cocoavillagemarina.com/

Day 13- July 2
Sailfish Marina- Stuart, FLA
http://www.sailfishmarina.com/

Day 14- July 3
Roland & Mary Ann Martins Martin Marina-
Clewiston, FLA
https://www.rolandmartinmarina.com/

Day 15- July 4
Fort Myers Yacht Basin- Fort Meyers, FLA
https://www.cityftmyers.com/381/Yacht-Basin

Day 16-22- July 5-11
Pine Island/St. James City, FLA
http://pineislandchamber.org/

Day 23- July 12
Labelle City Dock- LaBelle, FLA
https://www.citylabelle.com/

Day 24- July 13
Indiantown Marina- Indiantown, FLA
http://www.indiantownmarina.com/

Day 25, 26- July 14-15
Suntex Marina- Vero Beach, FLA
https://www.suntex.com/marina/vero-beach

Day 27- July 16
Titusville Municipal Marina- Titusville, FLA
https://titusvillemarina.com/

Day 28- July 17
Adventure Yacht Harbor- Daytona Beach, FLA
https://www.adventureyachtharbor.com/

Day 30- July 18
St. Augustine Municipal Marina- St. Augustine, FLA
http://www.staugustinegovernment.com/government/
general_services/municipal_marina/index.php

Day 31- July 19
Beach Marine- Jacksonville Beach, FLA
https://www.jaxbeachmarine.com/

Day 32- July 20
Fernandina Harbor Marina- Fernandina, FLA
http://www.fhmarina.com/

Day 33- July 21
Jekyll Island Marina- Jekyll Island, GA
http://www.jekyllharbor.com/

Day 34- July 22
Two Way Fish Camp- Brunswick, GA
no website; see FB

Day 35- July 23
Kilkenny Marina- Richmond Hill, GA
no website; see FB

Day 36- July 24
Shelter Cove Marina- Hilton Head, SC
https://www.sheltercovehiltonhead.com/

Day 37- July 25
Downtown Marina of Beaufort- Beaufort, SC
http://www.downtownmarinabeaufort.com/

Day 38- July 26
St. Johns Yacht Harbor- Johns Island, SC
http://stjohnsyachtharbor.com/

Day 39- July 27
Harborwalk Marina- Georgetown, SC
http://harborwalkmarina.com/

Day 40,41- July 28-29
Myrtle Beach Yacht Club- Little River, SC
http://myrtlebeachyachtclub.com/

Day 42- July 30
Seapath Yacht Club- Wrightsville Beach, NC
http://myrtlebeachyachtclub.com/

Day 43- July 31
Casper's Marina- Swansboro, NC
no website; see FB

Day 44- August 1
Oriental Marina & Inn- Oriental, NC
https://orientalmarina.com/

Day 45- August 2
Belhaven Marina- Belhaven, NC
http://www.belhavenmarina.com/

Day 46- August 3
Alligator River Marina- Columbia, NC
no website; see FB

Day 47- August 4
Pelican Marina- Elizabeth City, NC
http://www.thepelicanmarina.com/

Day 48- August 5
Waterside Marina- Norfolk, VA
https://watersidemarina.com/

Day 49, 50- August 6-7
Windmill Point Marina- Whitestone, VA
https://windmillpointmarina.com/

Day 50- August 8
Zahniser's Yachting Center- Solomons Island, MD
http://zahnisers.com/

Day 51- August 9
Port of Salisbury- Salisbury, MD
https://salisbury.md/port-of-salisbury

PHOTOGRAPHS

Alligator Canal

Along Came a Tiki Bar

Approaching a Lock

Approaching Belhaven

Approaching Daytona Beach

Approaching Lake Okeechobee

Approaching St. Johns Island, South Carolina

Approaching Two Way Fish Camp, Georgia

At Cape Charles Yacht Center

Beaufort, South Carolina

Belhaven, North Carolina

Below Wrightsville Beach

Blocked for painting

Caspers at Swansboro, North Carolina

Coinjock Marina

Converted Storage Space

Cosmetics and New Name Plates

Swamp Fox crossing the Neuse River near Oriental, NC

Crossing the Chesapeake

Day 1 on the Chesapeake

Dinghy Apparatus

Dismal Swamp

Downtown Norfolk, Virginia

Early morning storms on the Neuse River

En route to Cape Charles

End of Alligator Canal

Everything running perfectly!

Fish Cleaning Station at Two Way Fish Camp

Florida Cattle Ranch

Florida Rookerie

Gator Trout

Great Dismal Swamp

Hand Cranked Swing Bridge

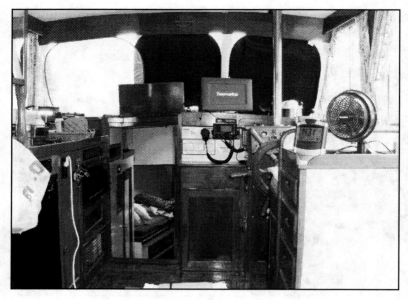

Happy for the AC!

Haul out for bottom paint

Hilton Head, South Carolina

Leaving Alligator River to Albemarle Sound

Much better looking!

Okeechobee stopover

Oriental, North Carolina

Placard leaving the Dismal Swamp

Rainy night in Georgia

Southbound Alligator River

Southern ties

Sunrise on the Chesapeake

Welcome at Solomons